Eraser

Eraser

written by

Bilal Baig, Christol Bryan,
Sadie Epstein-Fine, Marina Gomes,
Yousef Kadoura, Tijiki Morris,
Anthony Perpuse, and Nathan Redburn

Playwrights Canada Press
Toronto

First edition: March 2025
Printed and bound in Canada by Imprimerie Gauvin Ltée., Gatineau

Jacket art and design and interior illustrations by Cleopatria Peterson

Playwrights Canada Press
202-269 Richmond St. W., Toronto, ON M5V 1X1
416.703.0013 | info@playwrightscanada.com | www.playwrightscanada.com

Library and Archives Canada Cataloguing in Publication
Title: Eraser / by Bilal Baig and Sadie Epstein-Fine, with Christol Bryan, Marina Gomes, Yousef Kadoura, Tijiki Morris, Anthony Perpuse, and Nathan Redburn.
Names: Baig, Bilal, author | Epstein-Fine, Sadie, 1992- author
Description: First edition
Identifiers: Canadiana (print) 20240473949 | Canadiana (ebook) 20240473981 | ISBN 9780369104120 (softcover) | ISBN 9780369104144 (PDF) | ISBN 9780369104137 (EPUB)
Subjects: LCGFT: Drama.
Classification: LCC PS8603.A4424 E77 2024 | DDC jC812/.6—dc23

Playwrights Canada Press staff work across Turtle Island, on Treaty 13 and Treaty 20 territories, as well as unceded lands, which are the current, ancestral, and future homes of the Anishinaabe Nations (Ojibwe / Chippewa, Odawa, Potawatomi, Algonquin, Saulteaux, Nipissing, and Mississauga / Michi Saagiig), the Wendat, members of the Haudenosaunee Confederacy (Mohawk, Oneida, Onondaga, Cayuga, Seneca, and Tuscarora), and the xʷməθkʷəy̓əm (Musqueam), Sḵwx̱wú7mesh (Squamish), and səlilwətaɬ (Tsleil-Waututh) Nations, as well as Métis and Inuit peoples. It always was and always will be Indigenous land.

We acknowledge the financial support of the Canada Council for the Arts, the Ontario Arts Council (OAC), Ontario Creates, the Government of Ontario, and the Government of Canada for our publishing activities.

This one's for Isla Rose and Zevi Grace, the next generation.

For all the kids searching for some belonging.

For D. Bryan.

For Tanner, your spirit and passion continue to inspire every day.
You are loved and missed more than words can express.

To all the people reading this play, this is for you.

Eraser was first produced by Eraser Theatre and presented by Why Not Theatre's Riser Project at the Theatre Centre, Toronto, from May 7 to 14, 2019, with the following cast and creative team:

Performers: Christol Bryan, Marina Gomes, Yousef Kadoura, Tijiki Morris, Anthony Perpuse, and Nathan Redburn

Directors and Choreographers: Bilal Baig and Sadie Epstein-Fine
Dramaturg: Elise LaCroix
Stage Manager: Cole Vincent
Set and Costume Designer: Christine Urquhart
Lighting Designer: Rebecca Vandevelde
Sound Designer: Maddie Bautista
Assistant Sound Designer: Belinda Corpuz
Technical Director: Steph Raposo
Production Manager: Crystal Lee
Producer: Winnie Doyle-Marshall

How to Engage With the Book

Eraser is told from the perspective of six students in a sixth-grade classroom. They are all equally the protagonists. This book is laid out in a "choose your own adventure" style. It allows you to choose who your protagonist is and follow the story from their perspective. If you want to follow one specific character, look for a note at the end of the scene you're reading to skip to the next scene page that character appears in. You can read this book six times from six different perspectives. You can also read it from beginning to end and follow all of the characters' stories at the same time.

Staging Notes

Ms. Hall: Ms. Hall is not portrayed by an actor. Her presence is indicated through sound design. The audience should hear her footsteps.

Text: We have included additional text for this book that is not part of the staged play. If you are planning on staging *Eraser* you should remove that text from the script. Additional text is in THIS FONT so that it can be easily identified. In the staged play Tara's journal entries are spoken to the audience.

The simultaneous scenes in *Eraser* must have the same run time every performance and all scenes in the same block must run at exactly the same time. If you have a scene that is consistently running over time you should consider what text can be removed or if something else has to move slower. We trust your discretion. You can also contact the creators for consultation.

Movement: The movement in *Eraser* represents many things: the characters' fantasies, heightened emotions, forces outside of the characters' control, etc. The joyous moments should be truly joyous (e.g., "Synchronized Swimming," Noah and Eli's slow dance, Afroze's Bollywood fantasy). When the characters are expressing challenging emotions, the emotion should drive the choreography (e.g., "Feelings" and "Change Room A").

Bollywood: Bollywood is the only specific dance style in *Eraser*. The rest of the movement falls under the umbrella of contemporary movement but can be interpreted by each creative team. If you are staging *Eraser* you should engage a choreographer who practises Bollywood dance styles to choreograph Afroze's big Bollywood fantasy as well as the small Bollywood-inspired moments.

Performance Style: If you engage actors who are older than the characters in *Eraser* (eleven to twelve years old) it is important that they do not act younger than they are. They should not put on child voices. They should channel the feeling of being eleven or twelve while acting their own age.

We also welcome you to engage actors who are eleven and twelve. If you do it is important to consider the challenging content in the show and ensure the young people feel adequately supported.

Audience Interaction: Audience interaction is essential in *Eraser*. There are moments in the script when the audience is specifically asked to engage. However, what isn't written in the script are the small moments when characters invite their audience to sit with them at lunch, turn to them during an emotional scene, or make contact with them to share a private joke. These are things that you have to find in the room. Throughout the creation of *Eraser* we invited test audience members into our rehearsal room to give the actors practise in intimate interaction. These moments of connection will not happen unless the actors are given many opportunities to hone these skills in vulnerability and improvisation. As audiences entered the *Eraser* performance space they were divided between the six characters and invited to follow that character through the entirety of the performance. We also designated a space for audience members who were not able to physically follow one character. We curated a narrative for that section of audience, ensuring there was always a scene happening for them to witness.

Set and Costumes: There are no specific requirements for set or costumes, but it is important to note how rapidly the space in *Eraser* must change. There is no time for set changes because the audience is right there with the characters. Scenes must snap from location to location. In our production the only set pieces were six rolling office chairs and six scooters. The actors also must change into their swimsuits twice in the play. It is important that their costumes are easy to get in and out of during the choreography in "Change Room A" when they first undress. We recommend that the swimsuit is each actor's base layer to avoid full undressing.

Characters

AFROZE
"The New Kid"

ELI
"The Space Cadet"

NOAH
"The Sad One"

JIHAD
"The Follower"

TARA
"The Know-It-All"

WHITNEY
"The Queen Bee"

Non-Appearing Characters

Ms. Hall: Teacher
Alice Woo: Failed a grade
Nalisha, Daphne, Madeline: Cool girls
Marco: Cheeto fingers
Caleb: Noah's brother
Jahida: Jihad's sister
Manuel, Mateo, Iago, Christopher: Tara's brothers
Shamsu: Afroze's friend

Character Notes

In the original production of *Eraser*, Afroze was white and an Urdu-speaking convert to Islam. The character of Jihad was Arab Muslim. These characters must look visually different from one another in any production of *Eraser*, but they don't necessarily need to match the original casting. Casting actors who identify as Muslim or have a familiarity with Islam is strongly encouraged for both of these characters.

The character of Eli must be played by an East Asian actor.

The character of Whitney must be played by a Black actor.

The character of Jihad must be played by an actor with a disability.

The characters of Noah and Tara can be played by actors of any racial background.

You can adjust the text in the play to support your specific casting. You can also contact the creators for consultation if you're unsure.

1

Pre-Show

The characters are alone with each of their audiences before the show begins.

Eli

ELI: Today's gonna suck. Mmmmm, maybe it won't be that bad.

I'm actually a little stoked to be back. Like, it's gonna be cool seeing everyone again but I don't want to see teachers. They're boring and they suck! I feel like I haven't learned anything new in like five years! And my summer wasn't very summery. It was half boring because my moms are nurses and they're barely home and half of it was bad because this, like, thing happened. Anyway, I don't wanna learn—I wanna do, like, stuff, and learning doesn't feel like doing stuff, you know? Mommy Mel is all like, "Shhht! Pay attention, anak. If you fail, bahala ka." And Momma Zen is all like, "Sige, be like your tito, boy." Blah blah blah, fart fart fart. But no matter how hard I try, it's, like, still hard, ya know?

OH! BUT WE GET TO SWIM THIS YURRRRRR. Bruuuuuuuuuh. I don't even know how to swim, but I'm STOKED to try. It's gonna be nutso—McButso, bruh! Okay, I like school because of gym and recess and lunch and water fountains, but that's it. Hallways, libraries, the office, and learning are scuffed. Alsoooooo, I get to see Noah more now that we're in the same class. :) We're kinda besties and he's my favourite gaming buddy, but I haven't seen him in a few weeks because of a uhhhhh . . . the thing that happened . . . a bad thing that's you know . . . bleep bloop blap, oogity boogity, but yeah. It was bad. Anyway, we never talked much at school before but now that we're in the same class we gets to buzz buzz bees besties irl b. Woop woopti woop woop.

ELI does some sweet dance moves to accent the sound effects.

I hit him up a couple times, but he hasn't gotten back to me yet. Which is weird because he's normally quick with it. But you know, whatevs, eet eez what eet eez. Well, he's probably still thinking about . . . thingymabob. Whatevs though. Yabadabayolo!

He walks with a groovy bounce in his step.

Ughhhhh, okay, it's time to go to school. Wish me luck!

GO TO PAGE 17

Noah

NOAH: Hi, I'm Noah! My favourite colour is orange, my favourite number is twelve, my favourite animal is an elephant, because they never forget, and my best friend is Whitney. You're going to like Whitney, she's the best! She always dresses so cool, she makes up the funnest games, and she knows everything about everyone . . . and I mean EVERYONE! Ask anyone, they will agree that Whitney is the most popular girl in school. It's been so long since I've seen her—a whole summer! That's the longest we've ever gone without talking. It's not that I didn't want to talk to her, it's just that I couldn't because . . . I was just busy. The only person I really talked to or got to see was Eli, my best friend outside of school.

Me and Eli don't talk at school though, that would be weird. We've never been friends at school because we always had different teachers, and we can't just start talking to each other now? I already have a school best friend and besides . . . Eli changed this summer. He got weird. He's been messaging me for the last couple of weeks and I haven't been responding because, well, because . . .

Okay, can you keep a secret? I need you to promise me you're not going to tell anyone. My brother Caleb died this summer. He had heart failure that no one knew was going to happen, not even his doctors. He was really sick for most of the spring but then when summer came it seemed like he was getting better. He was allowed to play outside with me and we even went to the beach! That was so fun. I buried him in the sand and he took me to swim out to the FAR sandbank for the first time.

And then he was gone. I kept asking why they couldn't just give him a new heart and I still don't really understand why not? Oh my god, please keep this a secret. Please don't tell anyone about this. I don't want anyone at school knowing or asking me about it or talking about it to me or behind my back. I don't even want to think about it anymore. It's all I have been thinking about and I just need a break!

I wasn't going to say anything but I'm going to wear Caleb's jersey to school today. It was his favourite one. He is . . . was such a good hockey player. I found it folded up in a box at the bottom of his closet. I didn't want it to get dusty like all of his other stuff is going to. He'd hate that.

Okay, um . . . I have to go to school now.

GO TO PAGE 27

Whitney

WHITNEY: Hi, I'm Whitney.

Do you remember your dreams?

I have to tell you about this really cool dream I had the other night. I lived in the ocean and I was a cross between a mermaid and a whale. I definitely had a spout because I remember spraying all my tiny fish friends like it was a water park. I could go wherever I wanted. I was totally free to roam the entire ocean and go on any adventure. Anything was possible. I ruled the underwater realm.

Then I woke up and it felt like sludge filled my body because I realized I had to go shopping with my mom for a bathing suit. Even though I think it would be really awesome to be a mermaid or whale, or dolphin, or really any animal with a fin, I think swimming is stupid. We have to do swim class this year in school. I don't know why we couldn't stick to basketball and soccer or any other sport. It's not like I don't know how to swim, it's just embarrassing to be seen in front of everyone.

Honestly, I don't want to go back to school at all. I have Ms. Hall again, who is actually the worst. Somehow she chose me as her target and everything I do in class is wrong. It's not like I'm stupid or disrupt class. She actually has no reason to pick on me, but she always finds one.

The only good thing about going back is I finally get to see Noah again. Noah's been MIA for the entire summer because . . . well . . . something happened. He missed everything that happened. Like the thing with Maddy, Nalisha, and Daphne—he's gonna think it's so funny. Noah's basically the funniest person I know. He says the most hilarious things and he's the best at finding fun things to do at recess. I just really want my best friend back.

Well . . . I guess that's the cue. Time for school. Come with me?

GO TO PAGE 27

Afroze

AFROZE: Assalam'olaikum! Mera naam Afroze hai aur main bahot khush hoon ke aap sab mere paas bet rahey hain aur mere saath baatein kar rahey hain.

AFROZE laughs.

Your faces are really funny right now. I can totally speak English. Oh, I can totally speak Urdu too—that was the language I was just speaking—but I just wanted to see how you'd react if I . . . Uh, never mind, I don't know—I'm being weird.

Do any of you know languages other than English? Can you write "Hello" and "My name is __________" in your language or another language you know?

WRITE IT DOWN HERE!

....

....

Want to know more about the snacks I have? This is daal chana, it's lentils and spices and salt. Want to try some?

I'm from Pakistan. I was born there. My parents made us move here because my grandmother lives here, but she's getting too old to live by herself. I don't even know her. I mean I would get birthday cards, and my mother would talk about her. I don't know anyone here. I also don't really want to know anyone here. I just want to go back. Mostly I want to see my best friend. Last Eid her mother made some really good gajar ka halwa. It's like really mashed up carrots! I wonder what Eid will be like here. I'm Muslim but I think that maybe Eid will feel kind of different here.

Want to know what my best friend's name is? I made her name into a crossword.

1. Not to be too easy, but it is what two people who hang out and care about each other but aren't family are called.
2. The river where I have my favourite memories with my best friend.
3. This is the kind of vegetable that her mother used to make the halwa.
4. The last time I was with my best friend we went to our favorite river and I took a picture in my mind, and when I feel really lonely I think it, but because it's in the past it's a __________.
5. This is something that people might think if they think you might have done something. Like last year we took all of my best friend's big sister's makeup and exchanged it for crayons. Then we left her a note that said they would be brought back if she put two chocolate bars in a secret spot in front of our school. She thought it was us, but she couldn't prove it.
6. This is the language I was speaking at the beginning.

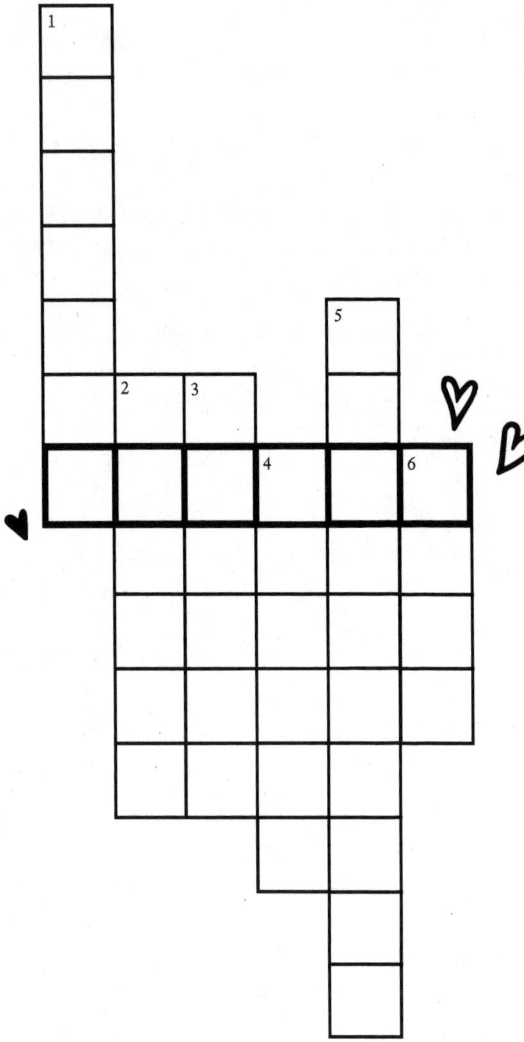

I miss everything a lot. I don't like it here. You don't have the Chenab River here. Oh, if you ever go to Pakistan, you have to see it. I think of my memories of Shamsu there every day and how we'd put our toes in the river for sooo long they'd get sooo pruney!

I have to start getting ready for school. I don't really care about rules, and I just want to feel like I'm at home in Multan again, so I've decided I'm going to talk in Urdu while I'm here. Can you please keep this secret?

Ab mujhe school pey jaana hai.

GO TO PAGE 27

Tara

TARA is in her room.

Tara: Hi, my name is Tara.
It is nice to meet you. Can I ask you something? Why do you think pencils come unsharpened? I mean, don't get me wrong, I actually enjoy sharpening pencils. I know it's weird, but I actually really like it because it's a really specific task that I can focus on. I just don't understand why some sets come unsharpened and some come sharpened. Do you know what I'm talking about?

Anyways, oh my god, I have to tell you— Can I tell you something else? Something really gross happened this summer . . . I went fishing for the first time! Apart from it being extremely gross, with the fish flopping in the air—and don't even get me started on gutting the fish we decided to keep—I realized how unfair fishing is for the fish. They must feel so much pain and most of time we don't even keep the fish. We just throw them back with a hole in their mouth. Overfishing is also a huge problem. Apparently soon a lot of fish species are going to go extinct.

Yeah. So I felt really bad for the fish, but then guess what? I caught the biggest one and my dad took a picture and my tia decided to cook it for dinner—gross, she's so gross. And then the rest of the summer my brothers tried to do better than me and they came close, but mine was the biggest. Yea . . . my family pretty much does everything together and I don't want this to sound braggy, 'cause it's just kind of what happens, but everything we do we always want to be the best at it. I mean literally everything.

That's why every September my mom has us write at least three goals to achieve by June. I'm not saying goal-setting isn't important—I love setting goals and focusing on getting them completed. I have really specific goals this year. I've listed them in order of when they're going to happen. One, get on the soccer team. Two, become class rep. Three, be helpful to others. I've listed that one last because I should just be doing it all the time. Starting now!

We need to help each other, you know? You know who needs a lot of help? Eli. I'm not trying to be mean, he just, you know, doesn't always get the homework. But he's so awesome in lots of other ways. Like he's really funny and he's really great to hang out with.

It's time for school! Let's go! And I wanna hear about your favourite summer moments or any goals you've got for this school year, so tell me on the way!

GO TO PAGE 27

SUMMER MEMORY / SCHOOL-YEAR GOALS

Jihad

JIHAD: Hey, my name's Jihad.

You know, I'm kinda excited. Not really for school or anything, but my sister bought me this new jacket and I wanna show it off. I'll show you when I start getting ready, but I just wanna be lazy right now.

My imam says I work really hard and I need to take more time to relax. Oh wait—do you know what an imam is? Basically a leader in the community who knows the Qur'an really well. And also leads all the prayers at the mosque.

Yeah, so over the summer I went to the mosque five days a week to help clean and set up the room, and pray, obviously. But during the school year I'll only go on Fridays because my dad says I'll be busy with a lot of homework this year.

I hate homework. I only like history. Ancient history. Or if there was a class on post-apocalyptic science-future stuff, I'd be into that too. Or if there was a pizza-eating class. Do you like pizza?

A couple of months ago I was fasting for Eid. Do you know what that is? It's a religious holiday that Muslims celebrate. I'm Muslim, did I say that already?

One time we were fasting, so like not eating food all day, and then when it was time to open our fast, our dad surprised us by making his famous pizza and we all ate that and it was the best. Yeah, my dad's pizza is famous. I was able to get his recipe, which you can use if you want.

I don't really talk about this stuff at school. Oh, I mean pizza I talk about all the time, but, like, the fasting stuff, or Eid, or going to mosque, or my imam, like all that stuff I just feel like I can't really talk about at school.

I don't know, like maybe it just doesn't feel cool, you know. And . . . This year, I really . . . Well, okay, there's this person at school named Whitney. She's really cool. I swear to Allah I don't have a crush on her. I just think she's really cool. Everyone thinks she's cool. Like I heard last year she read every book in the library about the ocean . . . like who does that?? Like, she knows everything. I think that's why she's . . . popular. Anyways, I'm just gonna talk to her. Like not right now, sometime soon. Like sometime this year.

Okay, gotta go! Gotta get to school.

GO TO PAGE 27

Easy Everyday Pizza

Ingredients:

- 3 cups all-purpose flour
- 1.5 tsp yeast
- 1.5 tsp sugar
- 1.5 cups lukewarm water
- Pinch of salt
- Olive oil
- Cheese (LOTS)
- Canned tomatoes
- Garlic, finely chopped (LOTS)

Dump your flour in a large bowl with a tablespoon of olive oil and a pinch of salt. In a separate bowl mix your yeast, sugar, and water and let it sit for five minutes. After five minutes mix your wet and dry ingredients in the large bowl by hand, being sure to coat your hands with a LOT of olive oil so the dough doesn't stick to your hands. Mix until the dough forms a thick elastic ball that bounces back slightly when you press a finger into it. Remove it from the bowl and roll it into a tight ball shape. Coat the bowl with olive oil before putting the ball of dough back in and covering it with a wet towel.

Let it rise for an hour, or until doubled in size.

While your dough is rising, heat your oven to 500 degrees Celsius. Then put your tomatoes in a hot pan with olive oil and the chopped garlic. Add spices if desired—hot chili powder and smoked paprika. Cook your sauce until it is thick and not all drippy and watery.

When your dough has risen, separate it into two balls. If you want to make one pizza wrap the second ball in plastic wrap and put it in the freezer for the next time you make pizza. Let the dough sit for ten minutes before using a rolling pin or glass soda bottle to roll it into a pizza shape. Take your dough (carefully so you don't rip it) and place it on either a baking sheet or an oven-safe frying pan coated in a thin layer of olive oil (this gives it a crispy bottom).

Now add whatever toppings you like, starting with the sauce (I like a saucy pizza). Halal pepperoni, or pineapple and olive, or zucchini. Then add cheese and put it in the oven until the top is bubbly and the crust is golden and crispy! Let it sit for ten minutes to cool down and enjoy!

2

Before School

NOAH: I don't think I'm ready to go back yet.

JIHAD: I hope everyone notices my new jacket.

AFROZE: Aur ab main school ke liye tayyar hoon.

TARA: I wonder if this year is going to be fun.

ELI: I told my moms I would look out for Noah at school.

WHITNEY: Ms. Hall, Bleh!

TARA: I can't focus on that right now, I have too much ahead of me.

NOAH: I don't want to talk about my summer. I don't want to even think about it.

ELI: I wonder what it's gonna be like to be Noah's best friend at school.

JIHAD: *(does a spin on the spot)* Ya!

WHITNEY: Plus swim lessons? Bleh!

AFROZE: Aur ab, main ja rahi hoon. Aao na mere saath!

Swimming Sequence

The students feel the distant wave coming. They hesitantly approach the ocean. They each dip a toe into the water. Some stay there, some step back. They each have to decide how they want to face the oncoming wave.

3

Gossip

Outside school, just before class.

Afroze

AFROZE: Why aren't we allowed in the school yet? There are so many rules here . . . I hate rules. Do any of you get into trouble a lot? What kind of trouble? Hey, let's try to crawl through some things—maybe those chairs? Let's go and pretend that we're spies and these are the rich people that we have to take the money back from. Like we're in an action movie with all the dishoom dishoom stunts and explosions for no reason!

Hey, I think he's looking at me—do you think he can hear me speaking English? Chalo, hum khel khelthey hain teekh hai? Yeh, yeh mera dupatta

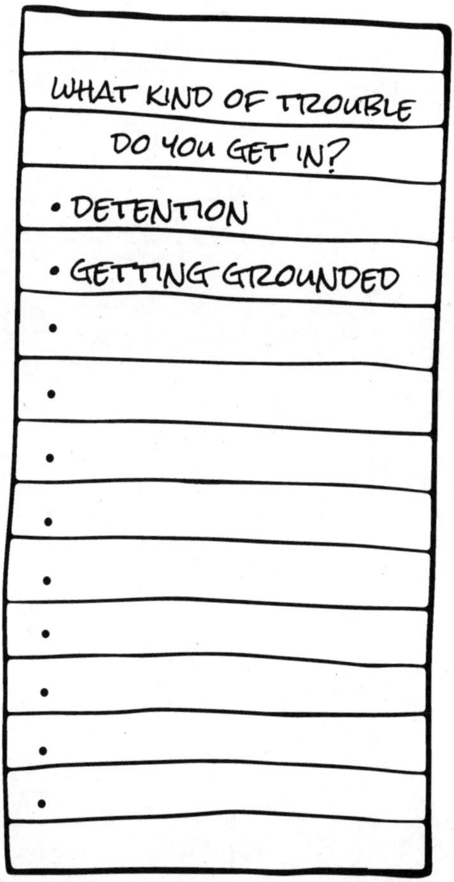

pakro aur aap bhi yeh pakro aur aap bhi aur aise aise karo acha? *[All right, let's play a game, okay? This is my duputta, you can hold this, you can hold this part, and then we can do these different things with it.]*

(plays with scarf) Wow, people here make it really obvious when they're talking about you . . . Woh ladki bahot baatein karti hain. *[That girl talks SO much!]* In Multan, in Pakistan, people talk about each other, but they just do it with their eyes. Like this.

AFROZE makes some silly motions with their eyes.

I had a feeling people might think I'm weird, so I don't really care what they're saying about me. I don't really care about this place, so it doesn't matter. Mujhe jaana hai yahan se, mujhe gahar wapas jaana hai. *[I want to leave this place. I want to go back home!]* Hey! Let's try to turn my scarf into a fort and see if we can all hide under it, okay?

AFROZE hides under their scarf fort.

Oh wait, look, what do you think is going on over there?

GO TO PAGE 42

Eli and Tara

ELI and TARA find each other.

TARA: Hey, woah. You're growing out your hair.

ELI: I am? Okay.

TARA: It looks really good on you—keep it. How was your summer?

ELI: It was okay. How was yours?

TARA: It was pretty normal. I went to my grandma's house a couple of times and went to a science camp for girls only and then went regular camping too, and tried fishing for the first time and I hated it.

ELI: Oh, wow, you did a lot!

TARA: Yeah, well, to be honest, I'm like pretty excited to be here. Don't tell anyone, okay?

ELI: Sure.

TARA: Especially Whitney.

ELI: I don't really talk to her . . .

TARA: I know, I'm just saying. Honestly, I just really want her to leave me alone this year.

ELI: Yeah, that makes sense.

Beat.

Hey so, good luck on the soccer tryouts.

TARA: Oh, thanks. I feel really ready. I've been practising for two whole weeks. My brothers have been giving me a lot of tips but, like, I pretty much know what I'm doing.

ELI: Hey, do you know that person?

ELI and TARA both look at AFROZE, who is looking at them.

TARA: Oh yes. That's Frozen.

ELI: Frozen???

TARA: Yeah. My mom's on the parent council and she knows all about the new students who come here and how to help them integrate in a safe and comfortable way. Frozen just got here like two days ago from Pak-ee-stan.

ELI: Are you sure?

They both kind of laugh.

What is she doing with her eyes?

TARA: I think she's a witch!

ELI: What do I do?!

TARA: Spin around three times and spit!

ELI does.

So did you hear about Caleb? Um, Noah's brother?

ELI: Yeah, um, I don't think we should talk about that.

TARA: Well, lots of people know about it. It was actually a topic at the parent council meeting last week, don't tell anyone. It's really sad. I'm actually really scared to talk to Noah cuz I don't know what to say. Do you know how his brother died?

ELI: Ya.

TARA: How? You don't have to tell me if you don't want to.

ELI: He had a heart thing.

TARA: How do you know?

ELI: Our families are good friends.

TARA: Oh, I'm very sorry for you and your family's loss, Eli. Sometimes it's so easy to forget how so many people can be affected by one person's death.

ELI: Um, actually, I'm just gonna go over and talk to Noah. Just wanna see if he's okay.

TARA: Oh my god, yes, that's a great idea, and please let him know how sorry I am.

ELI: GO TO PAGE 38
TARA: GO TO PAGE 42

Jihad

JIHAD is by himself but is trying to float around WHITNEY and NOAH, hoping to insert himself somewhere in their conversation.

JIHAD: Obviously Whitney and Noah find each other first. She's so cool. Like, those are the weirdest clothes and she pulls them off. I don't really know why she's friends with Noah. I mean, I guess after his brother died she kind of has to be. Oh, ya, his brother died this summer. My sister told me a few days ago. There was a letter sent out, she said I shouldn't read it because it's really sad. And also there's a new person here. I don't know what her deal is. Like, why is she wearing that? Clothing like that is not a costume. Seriously not cool. Wow. Check out Eli's moustache, it's almost as noticeable as Anthony's. Eli's really changed.

He used to be this super weird guy, you know. Which is why Tara's friends with him. She's kind of really annoying. And bossy. She just thinks she's really smart and better than everyone. But the truth is, she is really intimidated by Whitney. I mean, I guess we kinda all are—well not me, obviously. I didn't tell you this before, but I think Whitney and I could be really good friends. Like we're actually really similar. Like last year right before March Break she was walking down the hall and she dropped her history test and I saw that she got a really good mark on it and so did I—history's the only class I really love—and so I caught up to her and gave her back her test and said, "Keep up the good work," and she kinda laughed and since then we kinda started talking. Not really but kinda. Actually, I'm gonna talk to her right now.

OKAY, SO I'M GONNA ASK YOU SOME QUESTIONS, AND YOU CAN LET ME KNOW WHAT WOULD BE COOLER:

HOW SHOULD I START THE CONVERSATION WITH WHITNEY?

A) TELL WHITNEY I THINK HER OUTFIT'S COOL
B) TELL WHITNEY I THINK THIS YEAR IS GONNA BE AWESOME

HOW SHOULD I ASK IF WHITNEY WANTS TO BE FRIENDS WITH ME THIS YEAR?

A) ASK IF SHE AND NOAH ARE LOOKING FOR NEW FRIENDS
B) TELL HER THAT IT MAKES SENSE FOR US TO BE FRIENDS BECAUSE WE BOTH LIKE HISTORY

HOW SHOULD I BRING UP NOAH'S BROTHER?

A) CASUALLY ASK HOW NOAH'S SUMMER WAS
B) ASK HIM IF HE WANTS TO TELL ME THE STORY OF CALEB'S DEATH

JIHAD hangs around WHITNEY and NOAH's conversation from this point on until he can find the right point to jump in.

Noah and Whitney

NOAH: Hey!

WHITNEY: Hey! How's it going? Um, how's your family? Like your mom and dad?

NOAH: They're good.

WHITNEY: Oh. But . . .

Beat. Caleb's death is an unspoken tension between them.

NOAH: I love what you're wearing! It's so you.

WHITNEY: Ya, thanks. My cousin took me shopping last week.

NOAH: Cool.

WHITNEY: Oh my god, Tara the Terrible is still here. I was hoping she would've moved away over the summer. And since when did she and Eli become best friends?

NOAH: I don't know.

WHITNEY: Don't you talk to Eli and, like, go to his house and, like, go on family vacations together?

NOAH: Not anymore.

WHITNEY: Oh. Since . . . ?

NOAH: What? And why are you asking me like a million questions? How's *your* family doing? How's *your* mom and dad?

WHITNEY: They're . . . fine.

NOAH: Great.

Beat.

WHITNEY: Oh my god, why is she holding that soccer ball like that? Have you seen her run?

NOAH mimes TARA running. WHITNEY laughs.

Also, Eli is way too hot for her now.

NOAH: Ew. No. Eli isn't hot at all. Marco is.

WHITNEY: Ya, only if you're into permanently orange Cheetos fingers . . . Anyways, guess what? Madeline and Daphne and Nalisha aren't friends anymore. You missed the big fight because of—the thing you're dealing with—but it was at Nalisha's birthday party and it was really awkward and everyone had to leave early—and now none of them have friends because they were so exclusive before.

NOAH: Oh my god, maybe one of them can hang out with the ghost over there.

WHITNEY and NOAH look over at AFROZE and try to contain their laughter.

WHITNEY: Don't say that so loudly. Ghosts can curse you.

NOAH: That is such a big scarf it could be a blanket.

WHITNEY: It's a cloak.

NOAH: Or maybe it's like a magic carpet.

WHITNEY: No, that's stupid.

NOAH: Oh. Ya, I could totally see it as a cloak.

JIHAD joins the conversation.

JIHAD: Are you guys talking about the new kid?

NOAH: Ya.

WHITNEY: Do you know anything?

NOAH: Like what about those weird clothes?

JIHAD: Um, my mom wears clothes like that.

NOAH: Oh. Sorry.

JIHAD: That's okay. Hey by the way, Noah, if your family ever needed food or anything, my dad said he'd be happy to make some and I could drop it off?

NOAH: What?

JIHAD: Well just in case your parents aren't really cooking since your brother–

NOAH: Jihad, I don't want to talk–

WHITNEY: Oh my god, so I also heard the ghost is here alone. The rest of her family is back in Pakistan.

NOAH: Um, I don't think people in Pakistan look like that.

WHITNEY: Adoption?

NOAH: Do people in Pakistan adopt kids?

WHITNEY: I dunno.

JIHAD: I think so.

WHITNEY: Oh, hey look, it's Eli.

CONTINUE ELI'S STORY HERE!

ELI goes over to NOAH.

ELI: Hey. How are you doing?

NOAH: I'm . . . Fine?

ELI: Um, I was just wondering if you got any of my messages I sent . . .

NOAH: Um, yeah.

ELI: Oh okay—uhh maybe do you wanna talk after school or something?

NOAH: No, I'm okay.

WHITNEY starts laughing out of discomfort.

ELI: Well we can talk some other time. Maybe or something. Also, um . . . Caleb's / jersey looks—

JIHAD: Eli, don't you get it? Noah obviously doesn't want to talk about his brother dying / so can you just leave—

NOAH: JIHAD, oh my god, just stop . . .

Silence. NOAH *might burst into tears, so he leaves, pushing past* ELI.

(to ELI*, quietly as he walks away)* Thanks.

WHITNEY *scowls at both* ELI *and* JIHAD.

WHITNEY: *(to* JIHAD*)* That was really not cool, Jihad.

JIHAD *looks around, feeling incredibly embarrassed, and quickly leaves.*

4

Simultaneous Scenes

Feelings

NOAH, JIHAD, and ELI don't know how to express the big feelings they are having. At a loss for words, they move, trying to shut out the world. Their movements show what they are feeling inside.

NOAH is angry at JIHAD and ELI for bringing up his brother, Caleb, because he really didn't want to think about him. He can't believe school hasn't even started and he's already thinking about Caleb. He really wanted to avoid ELI, because he also doesn't know what to do with his big feelings for him. He calms himself down by tapping out the sound of Caleb's heartbeat. He doesn't want people to see how vulnerable he is, so he puts his attitude back on.

ELI is confused, hurt, and sad at how angrily NOAH reacted when he tried to talk to him. He tries to calm down—he doesn't want to show excess emotions—but his anger comes bursting through. He works hard to calm himself down again. He will NOT show his emotions at school.

WHAT MIGHT ELI BE SAYING TO HIMSELF RIGHT NOW?

WHAT MIGHT YOU SAY TO ELI IF YOU WERE WITH HIM RIGHT NOW?

JIHAD is embarrassed because he already screwed up his mission of being cool and becoming WHITNEY's friend. He really thought this year was going to be different, but he's in the same place he was last year. Even though he wants to give up he convinces himself not to freak out. He is going to try again.

WHAT MIGHT JIHAD BE SAYING TO HIMSELF RIGHT NOW?

WHAT MIGHT YOU SAY TO JIHAD IF YOU WERE WITH HIM RIGHT NOW?

ELI: GO TO PAGE 44
NOAH: GO TO PAGE 44
JIHAD: GO TO PAGE 44

Soccer Tryouts

WHITNEY and TARA run around the track for soccer tryouts. They do drills that test their ability to be on the team like dribbling, kicking the ball, and cardio exercises. WHITNEY is very good and TARA struggles but tries to keep a positive attitude.

WHITNEY: GO TO PAGE 44
TARA: GO TO PAGE 44

Bathroom Pondering

AFROZE: Mere saath aana hai? Aao na! Aajao!

AFROZE tries to figure out which bathroom to use.

Okay, I have to tell you something: I, I know what bathroom I'm supposed to use, but I kind of want to try . . .

Sometimes I think maybe I'll feel more comfortable in there . . .

AFROZE tries to explore what it might be like to go into the boy's bathroom.

Remember how I was telling you about Shamsu? She's the best because she loves to break rules and doesn't care if she gets into trouble. She—she told me as soon as I get here I have to write her a letter and tell her everything about this place . . .

AFROZE pulls out a letter they have started to write.

But I don't know what to say. I don't like it here. Sometimes I pray I could just go back. Actually, can you just hold this for me? Can you keep it safe? I just don't wanna think about it right now.

AFROZE hands the letter to the audience.

I should go back. You're good at keeping secrets, right? Can you please not tell anyone about . . . this bathroom stuff?

Um, thanks.

GO TO PAGE 44

5

Frozay's Intro

In the classroom. AFROZE *sits alone, silent.*

ELI *is still upset from the previous scene.*

TARA: Hey, Eli, I have a pencil for you.

ELI: Oh thanks.

TARA: Give it back to me at the end of class.

ELI: Thanks, Taradactyl.

TARA *makes dinosaur sounds.*

NOAH *and* WHITNEY *sit together.*

WHITNEY: So, Alice Woo totally failed a grade.

NOAH: No way.

WHITNEY: Yes way. That's why she knows everything.

NOAH: Ugh, she's so cool.

JIHAD: I bet you I'm going to have to show the new girl around. I don't know why they always make me do that for the new kids.

Ms. Hall walks up to AFROZE*'s desk.* AFROZE *tries to shrink. Ms. Hall has just prompted them to introduce themself.* AFROZE *gets up in front of the class. Everyone stares at them.*

AFROZE: Mera naam Afroze hai.

TARA: Can you say that in English?

AFROZE looks at Ms. Hall.

AFROZE: Mera naam Afroze hai.

TARA: I guess she hasn't learned how to speak English yet. I'm sure she'll learn soon enough. My parents did.

ELI: Oh cool, Miriam Afrozay. Do you think that's one name or two? It's pretty long if it's one name.

WHITNEY: Oh, I think "mera naam" means "name."

NOAH: Oh! So her name is Frozay!

WHITNEY: Heeeeey!

NOAH: Heeeey!

JIHAD: What language is that new girl speaking?! It's weird!

WHITNEY & NOAH: Heyyyy, Frozaaaay!

WHITNEY and NOAH laugh and do their secret handshake.

CONTINUE ON . . .

6

Cafeteria

AFROZE sits by themself and opens their lunch container. NOAH and WHITNEY sit together; JIHAD sits near them, and ELI and TARA sit near each other but at different tables with other people.

WHITNEY: Oh my god, what's that smell?

NOAH: I think it's Eli's.

ELI: What? / No, I have pasta for lunch.

TARA: *(to NOAH)* I'm sitting next to him and it's not from him.

JIHAD: Guys. It's . . .

Everyone looks at AFROZE. AFROZE looks at their food. Silence. WHITNEY and NOAH have some whispered banter before:

NOAH: Jihad, tell her.

JIHAD: / What?

TARA: Guys, I think she knows you're talking about her.

NOAH: Communicate in your language and tell her her food smells bed.

ELI: She obviously / knows.

JIHAD: We probably don't / speak the same language.

NOAH: *(to ELI)* I wasn't talking / to you, was I?

TARA: But, Jihad, you can speak Indian right?

WHITNEY: Um, don't you mean Hindi?

TARA: Jihad, is the language spoken in India Indian or Hindi?

WHITNEY: / Why are you asking about India if she's from Pawk-i-stan?

NOAH: / Oh my god, who cares, Jihad. Just go talk to her.

JIHAD: / Why are you asking me?

TARA: Aren't you from there?

JIHAD: No, I'm not. I'm from Michigan.

ELI: Man, stop lying.

NOAH: Jihad, PLEASE.

WHITNEY: Yeah, Jihad, could you talk to her?

JIHAD: Okay, fine!

JIHAD goes to AFROZE.

AFROZE: Assalam'olaikum.

JIHAD: Walekum'assalam.

AFROZE: Tum Urdu bol saktey ho?

JIHAD: Urdu? Oh no, I speak English.

AFROZE: Arbi bol thay ho? Arabic?

JIHAD: What? Uh, look, I just want to let you know that sometimes we eat in the hallways. We're allowed to do that here, it's kinda cool. I can show you.

JIHAD tries to point outside the cafeteria.

AFROZE: Nahi, shukriya, meh yahan pey teekh hoon. Aapko khana hai mere saath?

AFROZE offers their food to JIHAD.

NOAH: OH MY GOD!

WHITNEY: Oh my god, it looks like something died in it.

NOAH: Ya . . .

Beat.

JIHAD: Oh um . . .

AFROZE: Ley lo. Yeh saabzi ghosht hai. Kaana hai?

JIHAD: Oh uhhhh . . . I think I'm okay. My dad / packed a really big lunch for me.

Jihad, you should totally eat it. Right, Whitney?

WHITNEY: Ummm . . .

NOAH: YEAH, JIHAD, EAT IT. COME ON!

AFROZE: Likhen tum sab mere khaney ke baare mein / baat kar rahey thay, tho thoda sa chak lo?

JIHAD: Oh, um, uh that's nice– *(to NOAH)* OKAY!

JIHAD eats AFROZE's food.

A magic moment: JIHAD actually enjoys the food, so everyone experiences a moment of Bollywood joy.

JIHAD can sense everyone is watching him and he doesn't know how to react, so he leaves.

TARA: Jihad, go to the principal if you're really sick. The nurse isn't here today!

AFROZE goes to NOAH with the food. ELI laughs.

AFROZE: Tum bahot / baatein kartey ho, ab chup chap se kah lo. Teekh hai?

NOAH: Oh god, no! Frozay, go to Eli, please. / He really wants it.

ELI: WHAT? No I don't. Miriam, just stay in that corner with Noah.

JIHAD is out in the hallway.

JIHAD: (*to audience*) Okay . . . That was weird. Please don't tell anyone, but that tasted . . . good. Like the meat was chewy and the curry was like the perfect amount of spice. I had to pretend that it tasted really gross so no one thinks I'm weird. And also, she's still weird so . . . Wait, what's going on? Look!

TARA: You can have my sandwich. / I have an extra one.

AFROZE goes to ELI with their food.

AFROZE: Na na na, aap bhi, ley lo. Meri naani banaya. Bahoti acha hai.

ELI: No, I don't / want your food, thanks.

NOAH: No no no, Frozay, he really / wants to try it.

ELI: Noah, STOP. Why are you doing this???

WHITNEY: Okay, / Noah, maybe you should–

AFROZE: Meri naani bahot pyar se banaya. Kah lo na!

TARA: Here, take it, Afrozen. Seriously, my mom always packs me an extra one.

ELI: OH MY GOD, I DON'T WANT YOUR GROSS FOOD IN MY FACE!

ELI knocks the food out of AFROZE's hand.

Fantasy: AFROZE freaks out like they're in a Bollywood courtroom drama, screaming and pointing fingers as they demand justice.

AFROZE: Kya kiya?? Kyun? Yeh mera khana tha, aapka nahi . . . Kyun pekh diya?? Tum sab pagal ho. Tum sab janvar ho. Mujhe patha hai ke tum sab—KYUN MUJHE NAFRAT KARTEY HO??? KYUN KIYA? MUJHE BATHAO IS WAQT KUTHEY BEWAKOOF ULOO KE PATHEY!!!!!!!!

The fantasy ends.

AFROZE quietly picks up their food while everyone watches awkwardly. Then, AFROZE leaves.

TARA: Afrozen, you can have my—

WHITNEY: Keep your mayo sandwich far, far away, Tara.

Swimming Sequence

A wave crashes down on the students and they go underwater. The tide moves them, and they are unable to stay in control.

TARA notices the soccer list has been posted.

TARA: *(to audience)* The soccer list is up!

WHITNEY and TARA go check the soccer team list.

WHITNEY's name is on it. TARA's is not.

7 A

Simultaneous Scenes

Prayer Room (Jihad and Afroze)

JIHAD is moving chairs around, setting up the prayer room.

JIHAD: Okay, this is my favourite place in the whole school. It's actually just the extra-help room but every Friday I transform it into the prayer room. I always feel good in here. It's not the same as the mosque, but it'll do.

AFROZE enters while JIHAD is setting up.

AFROZE: Assalam'olaikum.

JIHAD: Uh, hey, sorry, I'm using this room right now.

AFROZE: Meh sirf dekh rahi hoon.

JIHAD: Sorry, I don't understand you. Do you understand what I am saying? This room is—

AFROZE: Haan likhen, meh soch rahi thi ke aaj meh namaz par sakti hoon yahan pey?

AFROZE steps further inside the space.

JIHAD: Uh, no, sorry, sorry, this space isn't for you. This is a prayer room and you can't watch while we pray.

AFROZE: Tho aap samaj thay ho ke meh musilmaan nahi hoon?

JIHAD: Yes. Muslim. For Muslims only. Not you. Please leave.

AFROZE sits.

AFROZE: Kyun soch thay ho ke meh musilmaan nahi hoon?

JIHAD: You're not Muslim. Muslims don't lie about being Muslim.

AFROZE: Meh jhoot nahi bol rahi hoon.

JIHAD: Can you stop talking to me in that language? It's not cool, okay? I don't understand you. I don't speak Urdu. I don't know why you're speaking what you're speaking, but I don't care because now thanks to you I have less than five minutes before everyone else comes in and I really need to finish setting up and this is really important to me.

AFROZE: Namaz mere liye bhi important hai.

JIHAD goes back to setting up. AFROZE is hurt and flicks their fingers in JIHAD's face.

JIHAD: GO TO PAGE 63
AFROZE: GO TO PAGE 64

Whales (Whitney)

WHITNEY looks around to make sure that nobody is looking and then sits down and takes a book out of her bag. It's about whales. She is consumed by it. She looks up to find she's being observed.

WHITNEY: This is the book I'm currently reading. It's really good. Don't tell anyone. I don't want anyone to make a big deal out of it, especially Tara, but I've basically read every book about ocean life in the library. You could call me an expert. I don't know why I like the ocean so much—it's just so big and there are so many creatures living in it that we know nothing about, and also . . . my grandma always talks about how magnificent the light is in the early morning when you're flying above it. This is my favourite book so far—it's about whales. Did you know that whales were actually tiny land mammals? About the size of house cats. They had fur, a tail, and everything. That was about . . . fifty million years ago. Eventually they started living near the water. I guess they wanted a change of life, to be different, to be seen as someone . . . something else. So they lived on land and in the water, like a crocodile. Then one day, two million years later—yeah it took two million years—they transformed. They grew gills, a spout, and they became the biggest creatures in the water. They're the rulers of the ocean.

Fantasy: WHITNEY enters the ocean and becomes the whale.

WHITNEY's fantasy is interrupted by everyone coming back from class. She doesn't want them to see what she is doing. She joins NOAH.

GO TO PAGE 63

Cleaning Up (Eli)

ELI searches for paper towel to clean up the mess left from AFROZE's spilled food. He checks to make sure no one is watching before he cleans it up.

ELI: Do you think paper will work? I got some in my binder . . . It's just spreading the mess around! Aww, geez. Yo, pass me that broom, please? What a waste. Man, being mean sucks. It wastes food!

He takes a whiff.

I actually really like the smell of this. It probably tasted real good too. Oh god, I'm so hungry.

He whimpers as he goes through his bag, pulling out a bag of chips.

Yummmmmm. Do you like chips? Hey, Noah's being a jerk, right? Like, I'm not going crazy, am I? I don't know, man, ever since the Caleb stuff happened he's been really moody. Like I get it, man, I miss him too. He was one of my best friends. I wish Caleb had two of those jerseys so I could've had one. They're pretty rad. Caleb was rad . . . Oh snap! Wanna see what he taught me once? It's called the buh-buh-buh broom bend. It goes like—this? I think.

ELI tries to broom bend with the mop but fails.

And like, uhhh. Nope. Oh, this is going terribly. I'm stuck! What's next?! WHAT DO I DO?!! CALL SOMEONEEEEEE—oh, nope, never mind, I'm fine, lol.

GO TO PAGE 64

Paper Crowns (Noah)

NOAH has three paper crowns cut out from his notebook that he is decorating. One is for him, one is for WHITNEY, and one is for you, the audience.

NOAH: Can you believe what happened at lunch? Not cool, not nice. This is what I meant when I said Eli got weird over the summer. He's acting out and he's super mean now. Don't you think? How can someone just bully the new kid? Truly awful.

Sometimes when a friend does something nice for me, I make them one of my special paper crowns to show them that they rule! I'm going to make Whitney one. I have extras if you want to make one for your best friends? I always write their name on it and decorate it however I think they would like it. Whitney will probably put hers in her binder and show it off in class. I hope Eli sees it.

Speaking of Eli, I know he was trying to talk to me earlier, and I know I kind of ignored him, but I do not want to talk to him . . . I don't know why. It's just this feeling that I have. He makes me so angry every time I see him, or he tries to bring something up about the summer or Caleb or about us being friends. Everything he says is just going to remind me of Caleb and how he's not here anymore and it makes me angry. He knows I don't want to think about it but he still does it. It's like he's doing it to hurt my feelings.

Like now I feel like wearing this jersey was a big mistake and I look stupid. Should I have just left it in the box and hoped I would forget about it? Maybe.

Okay, no more. I said I wasn't going to talk about it and I'm not going to anymore. I'm making a promise to you as my new friend that I'm done. Don't forget your crowns! Give them to your friends and make one for yourself. Everyone will know that you rule then! I can't wait to see it.

GO TO PAGE 71

1) Cut out the pieces of the crown.
2) Decorate!
3) Attach the strips of paper to the front piece and it's ready to wear.

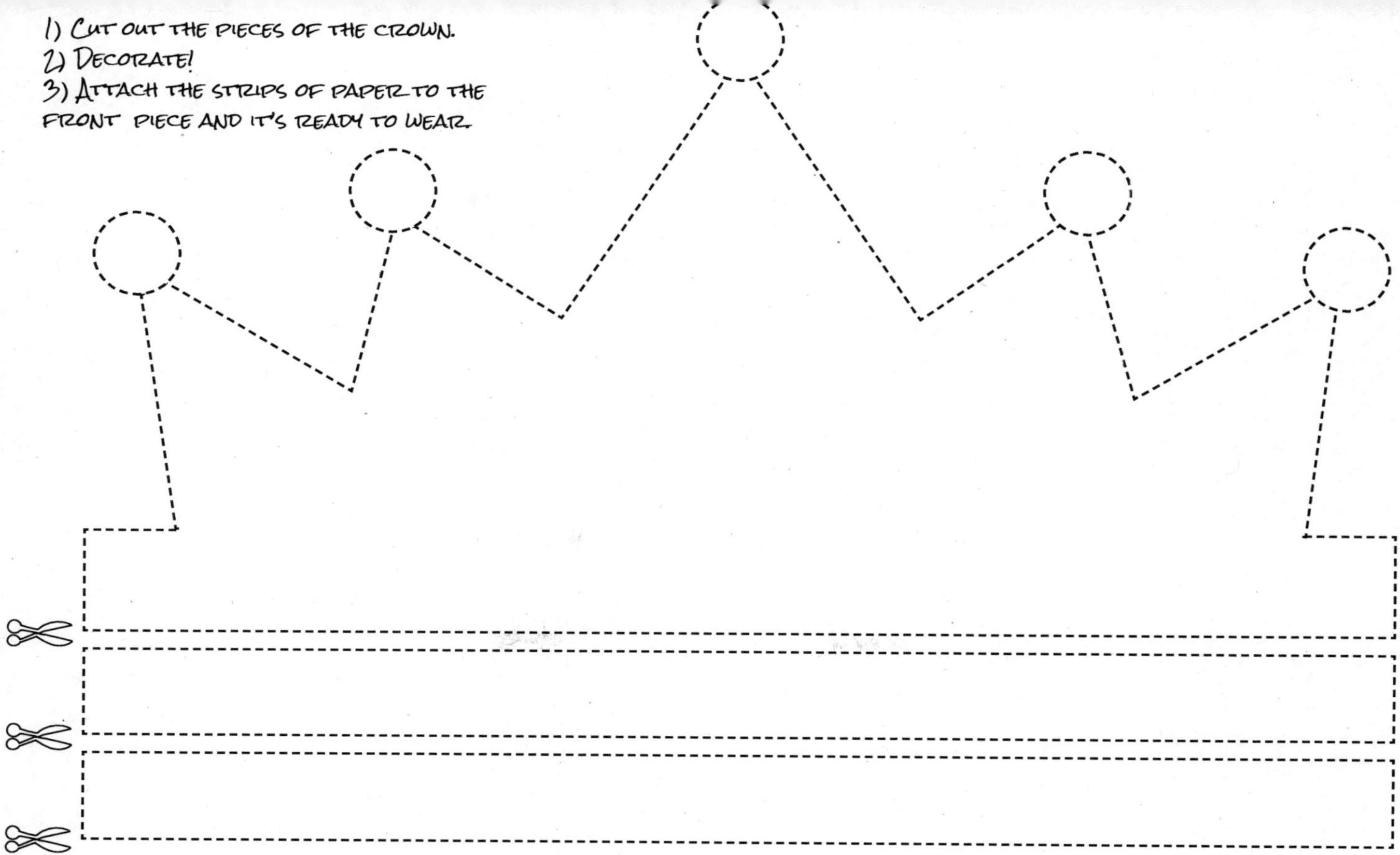

Drinking Water (Tara)

TARA sits, defeated with the news of the soccer tryouts.

She opens her backpack and takes a big drink of water. Her water bottle makes a noise. She pauses and takes another drink of water. She takes a deep breath, grabs her sandwich out of her bag, and eats half of it.

She takes another breath.

Tara: Can I tell you something? I actually play soccer all the time. We play it at my house. Actually, everyone in my family plays soccer. It's like a tradition for us. All my brothers have been on every soccer team ever. And when we play together, it's a lot of fun. They say I am not the worst at it. But actually . . .

She takes a deep breath.

I have fun when I play with my brothers. Or I used to. I never get to have fun. And now . . . It'll just be different. I guess I'm just different.

She takes another long drink of water.

This isn't how it was supposed to go. But I will just focus on my classes and that'll be okay.

HELP TARA OUT, THEN GO TO PAGE 64

WHAT ADVICE DO YOU HAVE FOR TARA?

7 B
Intro to School Projects

Everyone is on their way to work on their school projects. They meet up in the hallway in pairs.

Whitney and Jihad

WHITNEY: Can you believe I have to work with Tara on the project?

JIHAD: Well I have to work with the new girl who can't speak English.

WHITNEY: Oh my gosh! Ask if she's adopted.

JIHAD: Okay, I'll try.

JIHAD walks away.

WHITNEY: This is going to be the worst. Tara never stops talking and she always has to be the smartest one. She never lets anyone else answer questions even when they might know something better than she does.

WHITNEY: GO TO PAGE 65
JIHAD: GO TO PAGE 69

Tara and Eli

ELI: Sorry you have to work with Whitney on the project.

TARA: Thanks. I just hope she isn't too mean.

ELI: I don't really want to work with Noah either.

TARA: Ya, he's being really weird. It's probably because of his brother.

ELI: I guess . . .

ELI walks away.

TARA: Do you think he's cute? I never thought about it before, but I dunno. Something's different.

TARA: GO TO PAGE 65
ELI: GO TO PAGE 71

Noah and Afroze

NOAH: Um, hey. Frozay?

AFROZE looks at him

Um . . . Sorry about what happened at lunch. You know, like it sucks that Eli spilled your food.

AFROZE keeps staring at him.

Ya, um, so . . . ya. K, bye.

AFROZE walks away.

That was really awkward. Do you think she understood me?

AFROZE: GO TO PAGE 69
NOAH: GO TO PAGE 71

8

School Project

Tara and Whitney

TARA is reading the questions Ms. Hall assigned.

TARA: So how did you get to school today?

WHITNEY: I walked. How did you get to school?

TARA: My dad drives my brother Christopher to soccer and then I get dropped off at 8:25.

How did your family get to Canada?

WHITNEY: They took a plane.

TARA: From where?

WHITNEY: Antigua.

TARA: Oh wow. Where's that?

WHITNEY: It's a small island near the Dominican Republic.

TARA: Is it warm?

WHITNEY: Well . . . it's near the equator. So it's hot.

TARA: Did your mom and dad meet in Antigua?

WHITNEY: Ya.

TARA: My mom and dad met in Lisbon! Then they lived in Belém. Then they got a Canadian visa. They worked really hard to get here. They always say they worked that hard for my brothers and me. So now we've got to work really hard too.

WHITNEY: Ya, my parents too.

TARA: Have you ever been back to Antigua?

WHITNEY: Yeah, but I don't really remember it.

TARA: Do you remember anything?

WHITNEY: I remember flying over the Atlantic Ocean.

Shift: TARA and WHITNEY express their deepest truths through movement. TARA expresses how intense her parents' pressure is and how much of a burden it is for her. WHITNEY wishes she could escape her current reality and live in the ocean.

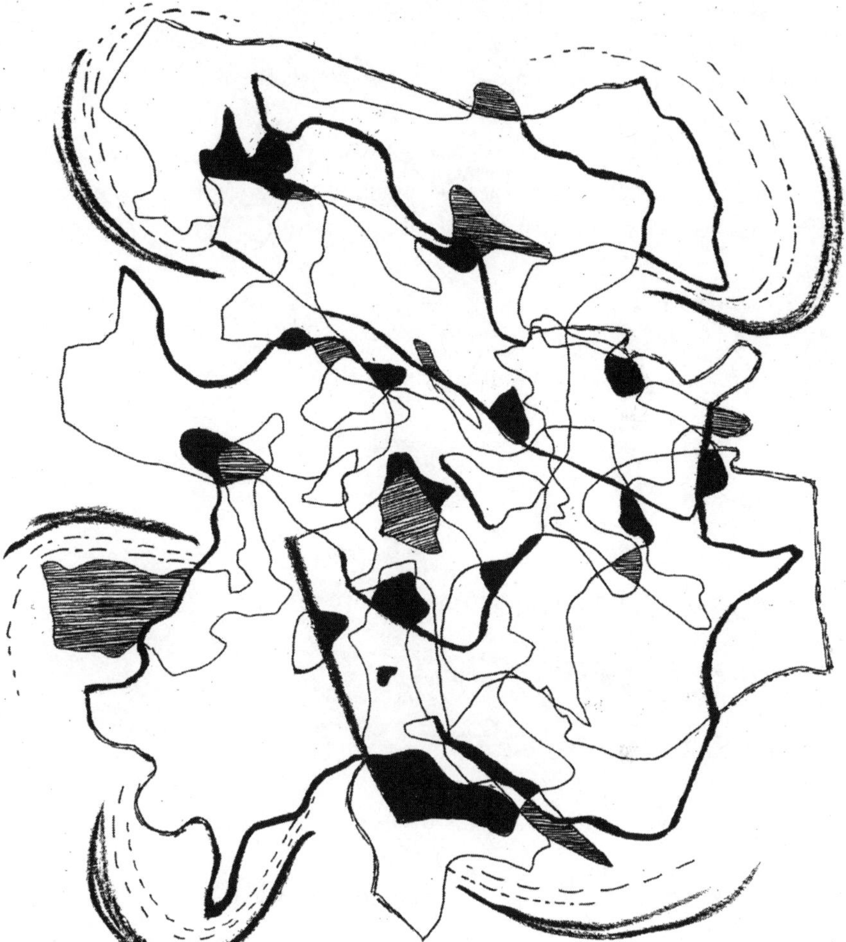

Shift.

TARA: What languages does your family speak?

WHITNEY: They speak English and they speak Patois.

TARA: My family speaks two languages too. When people come to my house and they hear my uncle speaking Portuguese they think that he's really angry, but he's just talking about the barbecue.

WHITNEY: My grandma always yells.

(imitating her grandma) Whitney! *Turn off the current!*

TARA: *(laughing and writing)* Yeah? And what else?

WHITNEY: What are you doing?

TARA: I think Ms. Hall is gonna really love this.

WHITNEY: No, you can't write that down.

TARA: Well, I have to present about you.

WHITNEY: Well you can use the other stuff. Not that.

TARA: Why? . . . Hello, are you going to answer?

WHITNEY: My grandma's really sick.

TARA: Oh . . . my vó died last year.

WHITNEY: Who?

TARA: My grandma. So, um, I get–

WHITNEY: I don't need you to get anything. Just use what you already have. I'm done.

WHITNEY: GO TO PAGE 76
TARA: GO TO PAGE 76

Jihad and Afroze

AFROZE is doodling henna designs in a notebook throughout the scene, and sometimes trying to write their letter to Shamsu as well.

JIHAD: So, did you understand anything Ms. said about the assignment?

AFROZE: Haan haan samaj liya.

JIHAD: Okay. So . . . For me, it all starts with my great-great-great-great-grandfather, who became the first imam of the vill–

AFROZE: Oh. Imam.

JIHAD: Yes. Great. Got it. Okay, so then decades and decades later my parents got married and my mom got to Michigan first and worked hard to sponsor my dad so they could have my sister, Jahida, who is kinda like a third parent to me, which–

JIHAD can see AFROZE really isn't listening.

Okay, yeah so that's pretty much it. Are you adopted?

AFROZE: Nahi.

JIHAD: Okay, then how did you get here?

AFROZE: Faida kya hai?

JIHAD: Okay, here, why don't you show me . . .

JIHAD draws North America.

Here's Canada, and here are the States. Where is your family from?

AFROZE: Arey yeh sirf do mulk hai, yeh pura duniya nahi hai.

JIHAD: Duniya? No, we're not talking about the whole world–

AFROZE: Aap Arbi samaj thay ho?

(recites Arabic passage) Inna lillahi wa inna ilayhi raji'un.

Yeh mera favourite sura hai Qur'an mein!

JIHAD: Why are you speaking to me in Arabic? Just stop. Just show me where your parents are from, and don't say Pakistan!

Shift: JIHAD and AFROZE express their deepest truths through movement. JIHAD feels embarrassed and ashamed that he doesn't speak Arabic and he wants to know how to speak it. AFROZE misses Pakistan so much.

SEE PAGE 67

Shift.

AFROZE: Acha dekho . . .

AFROZE begins to draw in their notebook.

Yeh Canada hai . . . Yeh USA . . . Yeh dusra jaga . . . Yeh Europe . . .

JIHAD: Oh, Europe, okay–

AFROZE: Yeh Africa, / yeh Asia . . .

JIHAD: No no, not Africa.

AFROZE: Yeh Australia . . . Aur yahan pey Hindustan aur Pakistan. Aur ek naani nana Europe mein hain aur ek daadi dada Canada / mein aur doosrey–

JIHAD: Okay, so Canada and Europe. I think I've got enough for you.

AFROZE: Meh Pakistan / mein peda hua aur meh gyaara saal wahan pey rehthi thi.

JIHAD: Okay, and I just forgot to mention that though I haven't been to Lebanon, I'm Lebanese because of my family history. I can't just make that up.

Beat.

Just ask me any questions if you're confused. I really don't want to be stressed out during the presentation. Thanks.

JIHAD: GO TO PAGE 76
AFROZE: GO TO PAGE 76

Noah and Eli

An awkward silence. ELI *is fidgeting.*

NOAH: Are you okay?

ELI: I just don't really want to be here.

NOAH: Ya, well, me neither.

ELI: No. Ugh. I mean I'd rather be outside or something.

NOAH: Okay.

ELI: Whatever. We have to pass this, so let's just do it.

NOAH: So I basically know everything about your family already. I know that your moms came from the Philippines and then made you.

ELI: Yeah, well, did you know my tito Rick is my biological dad?

NOAH: WHAT?!

ELI: Yà.

NOAH: You mean your uncle who always wears the hat?

ELI: Yup.

NOAH: That's how gaybies are born?

ELI: I mean that's how THIS gayby was born . . .

NOAH: Maybe that's what you got from him.

ELI: What?

NOAH: The hat. I haven't seen you take yours off in years.

ELI: Oh, uh, I guess . . .

NOAH: Do you ever wish Rick was your actual dad?

ELI: Oh, uh, I mean . . . I dunno . . . no.

ELI no longer wants to talk about his family.

So I know that you and Caleb were born in Toronto.

Shift: ELI and NOAH express their deepest truths through movement. ELI doesn't know if he wants a dad or not, but he feels like he's betraying his moms if he says he does. Sometimes he thinks it would be good to have a dad to talk to. NOAH feels that his family tree is broken since Caleb died.

SEE PAGE 67

Shift.

But, like, where are your parents from?

NOAH: Yup. They were also born in Toronto.

ELI: Oh, cool, so like you're not from anywhere else?

NOAH: Well, my grandma on my mom's side is from Sicily. And my grandpa is from Alsace, Germany. My grandma on my dad's side is Irish and my grandpa on my dad's side is English and Scottish.

ELI: Woah, so that makes you like five things. Six if you include Canadian!

NOAH: Ya, I guess. I never thought about it like that.

ELI: Ooohhhhh, is that why we learned the Irish jig thing at the cottage?

NOAH: Ya, it's really important to my grandma. They put Caleb in Irish dance lessons when he was younger.

ELI: We should totally teach it to the class!

NOAH: No. It was Caleb who was good at it, not me.

Pause.

ELI: Oh . . . Do you want me to mention Caleb?

NOAH: Yeah, I don't know yet.

ELI: I've been meaning to tell you: Caleb's shirt looks dope on you.

An awkward pause.

We can show the class the tinikling!

NOAH: The what?

ELI: The stick dance! Remember? That dance that my moms taught us at the cottage during the summer?

ELI begins a rhythm and NOAH attempts to keep up.

Here, let me show you.

ELI takes NOAH's hands to show him the rhythm. They both pause, holding hands. After a moment NOAH breaks it off:

NOAH: Yeah, let's do that. Okay, we're done here.

NOAH: GO TO PAGE 76
ELI: GO TO PAGE 76

School Project End

WHITNEY gets up to walk away from TARA, but Ms. Hall approaches. The entire class watches.

WHITNEY: Ms., I wasn't doing anything. She's the one who— No, I don't want to repeat what happened last year . . . No, I don't want to sit in the corner. But I have soccer practice after school. Fine, I'll see you then.

CONTINUE ON . . .

9

Change Room

All of the students have to change into their swimsuits. They all carry insecurities about their bodies and being undressed in public, so they try to be as concealed as possible. They awkwardly remove their clothes.

Fantasy: Their shirts begin to strangle them and they desperately need to remove them, but they don't want to. Finally, they remove their shirts. The moment they do it's like they've broken the surface of the water and they all take a big gasp of air. They are wearing their swimsuits.

The students remove the rest of their clothes and put on their goggles.

10
Swim Class

The students stand at the edge of the pool in their bathing suits, exposed and uncomfortable.

Fantasy: The students all behave how they would like to in the pool. AFROZE *sits on the edge, dipping their feet in;* WHITNEY, NOAH, *and* JIHAD *get into a water fight;* ELI *jumps into the pool a million times.* TARA *watches the rest while they play. Her fantasy involves all of her classmates.*

TARA: All right, everyone, positions!

All the students assume their synchronized swimming positions. They perform a beautifully choreographed routine that is up to TARA*'s standards.*

The fantasy ends. The students are back in the harsh lighting and reality of the swimming pool. AFROZE *is staring at* JIHAD*'s leg.* ELI *takes a deep breath and holds it.*

JIHAD: *(to* AFROZE*)* What are you looking at?

AFROZE: Kuch bhi nahi.

JIHAD: Do you want to know how I became disabled? I was in an epic sword battle with my cousin. They were supposed to be fake swords, but by the time we found out they were real swords it was too late.

TARA: Come on, Jihad, don't be dumb. Tell her what actually happened.

WHITNEY: No, I think it's great. Much better than the shark or bear story.

TARA: All right, I'll tell you, Frozen. He actually–

JIHAD: It's my story, Tara. She doesn't understand us anyways, so what's the point?

WHITNEY: But if we talk to her in English that's how she can learn.

A whistle blows and they know it's time to get into the pool. They all get in. Some feel cold, some are more comfortable in the pool once their body is immersed in water. They begin doing laps including front crawl, breaststroke, and back crawl. They decide to have a race. WHITNEY almost wins the race, but JIHAD physically stops her. This begins a wrestling match that NOAH and ELI are dragged into. It ends with ELI kicking NOAH in the neck.

There is a moment where nobody knows what to do, then they all swim to finish the race. ELI wins. TARA comes in second.

ELI runs through the water in victory. TARA runs over to ELI and kisses him while everyone else stares at them. AFROZE goes back to the change rooms because they think everyone is stupid. Annoyed, WHITNEY also leaves.

ELI: GO TO PAGE 81
TARA: GO TO PAGE 82
NOAH: GO TO PAGE 84
JIHAD: GO TO PAGE 85
WHITNEY: GO TO PAGE 86
AFROZE: GO TO PAGE 86

11

Simultaneous Scenes

Never Been Kissed (Eli)

ELI: :O

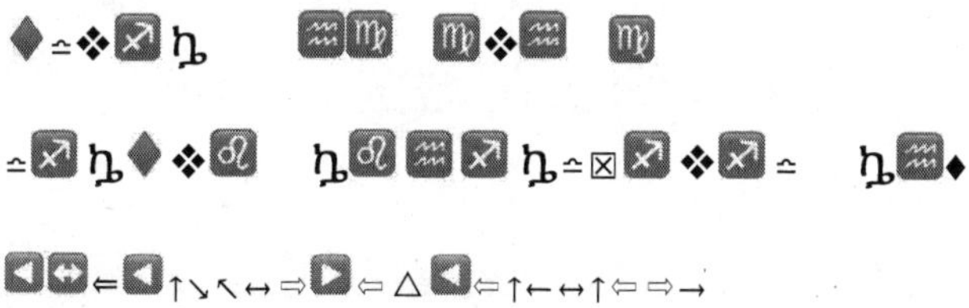

WHAT THE HECK WAS THAT? WHAT DO I DO?

Gyyyyyyahhhhhh, I dunno, man! Like, I really have no idea. Okay okay okay okay, let's chill, take a beat. STRETCH! BREATHE! Nope! Didn't help.

Or my gorsh, I dunno guys. Like tbh, I kinda liked it, but I mostly hated it? And I think I kinda didn't like it because I think I kinda like someone else . . . I think. I don't know! I'm so confused! Like is she my girlfriend now? Is that what that means? That's insane! Does Tara even wanna date me? I dunno man, I just wanna be friends, but I don't want to be mean either. Why did she do that?!

I've never been kissed before.

GO TO PAGE 88

Feeling Nothing (Tara)

Tara: That was weird, right? I don't know why I did that. I mean, why did I do that? Oh my god—what does it mean now? It didn't feel, no . . . it didn't feel like anything, no, no . . . that's not right, it's that, I didn't feel anything . . . And I guess I just thought you're supposed to feel something when something like this happens. I don't know what I'm talking about.

I should just be focusing on school. I don't know why I'm distracting myself . . . This is not really like me. Can I tell you something? I won the Attentive Listening Award last year.

Except . . . well, the truth is while the principal was giving her speech, I wasn't really listening. They already told me I was gonna win the award! So . . . I didn't stand up right away when she called my name. But that was because I was thinking about my future, and how this award might help me . . .

And how it might make my parents happy and how my tia would make such a big deal, even though she wouldn't understand it . . . but for sure my vó would've been really proud if she was here. Ugh, this must be a really hard time for Whitney—losing a grandma is so not easy. If Whitney and I were friends maybe I could . . . Well, maybe I could . . .

TARA pauses to think and then snaps up in attention.

Sorry, that was random. Let's just pretend I never kissed Eli. Can you promise me you won't tell anyone else what happened? Let's make it an official deal by doing a secret swap. I've told you a secret, now you tell me one.

GO TO PAGE 88

WRITE A SECRET TO SHARE WITH TARA

Ice Pack (Noah)

NOAH is holding an ice pack to his neck.

NOAH: He kicked me in the neck!! Now I have to walk around all day with this big ice pack on my neck. How am I going to do anything?! I can't believe Eli would do something so low as to cheat and hurt someone just so he could win and kiss Tara. Of all people, TARA! Tara the Terrible. Who does that? We have a hands-off policy at school and I'm pretty sure that means feet too.

I'm not surprised he did that, though. He's always looking for attention. One time Nalisha had a pool party and everyone was invited, even Tara, and she showed up in this awful bathing suit . . . for attention, just like Eli. Anyways, Nalisha, Alice Woo, and I were doing water routines and making up dances. Whitney had to watch because she wasn't feeling well . . . probably because of Tara's bathing suit. So there was a part in the routine where I had a solo and I was going to show everyone my triple axle kickstand round off. It was like something out of a movie. Just as I was about to start, Eli was getting people to dare him to do a cannonball. When he jumped in it made such a big splash that all of these big waves happened and knocked me off balance and I hit my leg on the bottom of the pool. I was in so much pain I had to be carried out of the pool.

But then Nalisha's mom gave me this really delicious passion-fruit popsicle to make me feel better, and I was the only one who got one, and then suddenly my leg just didn't hurt anymore, and everyone felt really bad for me.

Ugh, this ice pack is getting too warm and I need a new one. Some advice, make sure you have an ice pack with you to give your friend if they ever get kicked in the neck.

GO TO PAGE 88

Cool Kiss (Jihad)

JIHAD: Oh my gosh. I've never seen someone do . . . *that* before. My imam says we can't do that until we're a little bit older. You know, this week, my imam was giving this talk and he was talking about the Prophet Muhammad and his first wife, Khadijah. She was really rich and he was a poor shepherd. She had a lot of suitors, but she didn't like any of them because they just wanted to marry her for her money. But then she met Muhammad and she fell in love with him because he was really nice and honest and he probably spoke Arabic really well too. After they got married he got so much cooler! That's when he discovered Islam. The angel Gabriel came to him and told him about the Qur'an and told him that he was going to be a prophet. Even though Khadijah loved him before, she loved him even more once he became a prophet because, like, how cool would it be to be a prophet. They made out all the time.

I wonder what getting kissed felt like for Eli? Did he think it was cool, or . . . Wait. What do other people think? Like, is it cool to be kissed? In a pool? Like, what does Whitney think about it? Is Eli cool now? Is Tara cool now? What do you think?

DO YOU THINK IT'S COOL . . .

A) TO KISS SOMEONE
B) NOT TO KISS SOMEONE

DO YOU THINK IT'S COOL TO KISS . . .

A) IN A POOL WITH ALL YOUR FRIENDS WATCHING
B) ALONE WITH NO ONE WATCHING

DO YOU THINK GETTING KISSED FEELS LIKE . . .

A) A WET EEL
B) A FLUFFY CLOUD

GO TO PAGE 88

Bonding Time (Whitney and Afroze)

WHITNEY and AFROZE enter the change room.

WHITNEY: OH MY GOD, that was the grossest thing ever. It was so aggressive, like two betta fish kissing.

AFROZE nods then makes fish lips and begins to aggressively kiss the air around them. WHITNEY tries to mask her amusement.

Oh my god, you are so weird, Frozay.

AFROZE stops kissing the air.

Beat.

AFROZE: Hey, actually, it's Afroze.

WHITNEY: Oh, whoa, you learned English fast.

AFROZE: I've actually always been able to speak English . . .

WHITNEY: Oh . . . Then why–

AFROZE: I don't know. I just don't want to be here, so I'm . . . pretending . . . to be somewhere else. I think. I know it's weird, sorry.

WHITNEY: No, don't worry. It's cool that you do whatever you want. Speak whatever language you want.

Beat.

You know, if I could be somewhere else, I would. Where would you want to be?

AFROZE: The Chenab River. It runs through Multan, in Pakistan. Or the Arabian Sea.

Fantasy: WHITNEY and AFROZE become sea creatures. They swim around and play together.

WHITNEY: GO TO PAGE 88
AFROZE: GO TO PAGE 88

12
Change Room

TARA enters the girls' change room.

WHITNEY and AFROZE's fantasy is interrupted.

TARA looks at them like, "What is going on?" AFROZE pretends that they are finishing a stretch, trying to be normal when that ship has totally sailed.

AFROZE: Ah . . . Stretch—stretch . . . Good.

A long, awkward silence.

ELI enters the boys' change room, followed by JIHAD, then NOAH. Silence. No one wants to bring up what just happened. NOAH gives in.

NOAH: So did you enjoy that?

Silence.

In the girls' change room:

WHITNEY: Was Eli's mouth super dirty?

TARA: No.

In the boys' change room:

NOAH: Did you?

ELI: I don't know what you're talking about.

In the girls' change room:

WHITNEY: So it was super clean.

TARA: No.

In the boys' change room:

NOAH: Yeah you do. Jihad, you saw, right?

JIHAD: Oh, um, yeah. I think so.

In the girls' change room:

WHITNEY: Well that's gross.

In the boys' change room:

NOAH: So, do you like her?

In the girls' change room, AFROZE *starts to focus on their chest. They aggressively try to flatten themself out.*

WHITNEY: So did you like it?

In the boys' change room:

NOAH: Oh my god, you totally like her.

In the girls' change room:

TARA: It was okay.

In the boys' change room:

NOAH: I knew it.

ELI: Can you leave me alone?

NOAH: Can you stop kicking people in the neck just so you can make out with your girlfriend?

In the girls' change room, AFROZE *enters a fantasy. They are looking at themself in the mirror, examining themself from all sides.*

AFROZE: I wish this would stop. I never want to change.

AFROZE *aggressively tries to flatten out their chest. The others join in, trying to erase parts of themselves they don't like. The fantasy ends.*

TARA: Afrozen, what are you doing?

AFROZE *stops flattening out their chest.*

In the boys' change room:

ELI: She's not my girlfriend.

NOAH: Yeah? Then why were you putting your tongue all over her face?

In the girls' change room:

WHITNEY: So are you two dating?

TARA: No. I don't think so.

WHITNEY: When you kiss someone, it basically means you're dating, right, Afroze?

AFROZE doesn't care. TARA doesn't think AFROZE understands.

In the boys' change room:

ELI: I didn't kiss her. I don't know what it means, okay?

NOAH: It means you two are dating now. Doesn't it, Jihad?

JIHAD: Oh, um, yeah, I think so.

In the girls' change room:

TARA: Look, I don't wanna talk about this. It's not a big deal.

In the boys' change room:

ELI: This is so stupid.

NOAH: It's not stupid, it's just true.

ELI: What then? What do I do?

NOAH: I dunno. Ask your friends.

ELI: What do you even know?

NOAH storms out.

In the girls' change room:

WHITNEY: You know he's shorter than you.

TARA: Um, by like a few centimetres.

In the boys' change room:

JIHAD: So do you feel different now?

ELI: What?

JIHAD: You know, when you put your mouth on hers—

ELI: Jihad, seriously?

In the girls' change room:

WHITNEY: So . . .

TARA: So?

WHITNEY: Soooo . . .

TARA: What?

WHITNEY: What?

TARA: What??

In the boys' change room:

JIHAD: Sorry—I was just . . .

In the girls' change room:

WHITNEY: *(whispers)* Penis.

TARA: OH MY GOD, DON'T SAY THAT.

In the boys' change room:

JIHAD: It's just the last time I kissed a girl it was pretty—cool—um, so I was just wondering if your experience was pretty cool or not?

ELI: If I answer, will you leave me alone?

JIHAD: Yes.

In the girls' change room:

WHITNEY: *(a little louder)* Penis.

TARA: Seriously. I'm being serious right now.

In the boys' change room:

ELI: Okay. Yes. It was pretty cool.

In the girls' change room:

WHITNEY: PENIS!

TARA bursts into laughter.

TARA: PENIS!

WHITNEY and TARA proceed to play the penis game. AFROZE witnesses.

In the boys' change room:

JIHAD: Do you want to kiss her again?

ELI: Oh my god, Jihad, I don't know!

JIHAD: I've heard that, like, if you close your eyes you can imagine the person you want to kiss.

ELI: So?

JIHAD: So when you close your eyes, do you picture Tara?

In the girls' change room:

AFROZE can't contain it anymore.

AFROZE: PENIS!!

WHITNEY and TARA are stunned.

In the boys' change room:

ELI: I don't picture anyone. This is weird, Jihad.

JIHAD: Ya, okay. Okay. See you later.

JIHAD leaves as NOAH comes back in.

We enter a fantasy:

NOAH: Hey.

ELI: Hi.

NOAH: Can I talk to you?

ELI: Why?

NOAH: I know you're mad at me. Because I haven't been nice to you. And I know you didn't mean to kick me in the neck. It didn't really hurt, I just overreacted.

ELI: Why are you saying all this?

NOAH: Because I'm sorry. Okay? And I guess I was just jealous that you kissed Tara . . . and not me.

The fantasy is interrupted.

Hello?? Eli?? HELLO???

ELI: Wow, what?

NOAH: YOU'RE SITTING ON MY HEADPHONES. GET OFF.

ELI: WHATEVER!

ELI jolts up and NOAH grabs the headphones from where ELI was sitting. ELI shoves NOAH to go away, which shocks them both. NOAH storms off and ELI grabs his things and leaves as well.

In the girls' change room:

TARA: Wow. I didn't know they played that game in Pak-ee-stan.

WHITNEY rolls her eyes. They both wait for AFROZE's response.

AFROZE: I've never played it before. The rules of the game seemed pretty obvious.

TARA: You can speak English?!

WHITNEY rolls her eyes and shakes her head.

AFROZE: Yes.

TARA: Oh. Why? I mean, if you could speak–

AFROZE: I don't know.

TARA: Okay, but if you could–

AFROZE: Sometimes I just want to be back in Pakistan.

TARA: Okay, but none of us speak that language, so why don't you just speak English?

Pause.

AFROZE is hurt by this. AFROZE quickly grabs their things and leaves. WHITNEY looks at TARA then leaves as well. TARA is confused, then slowly leaves.

Swimming Sequence

The students desperately want to get out of the water. They are trying to find the surface, trying to find air. They are drowning.

WHITNEY: GO TO PAGE 98
AFROZE: GO TO PAGE 98
JIHAD: GO TO PAGE 101
TARA: GO TO PAGE 103
ELI: GO TO PAGE 106
NOAH: GO TO PAGE 108

13

Simultaneous Scenes

Lost and Found (Afroze and Whitney)

AFROZE stumbles upon the lost and found. They have no idea what it is. They start to play around with some of the items and ends up holding two men's hats. WHITNEY catches them.

WHITNEY: Try that one on.

AFROZE: What?

WHITNEY: Well, you like to wear a lot of colours, so that hat could contrast your wardrobe in a cool way.

AFROZE: Oh . . . But I can't take it.

WHITNEY: Sure you can. Finders keepers. The things in that bin are the forgotten ones. They'd love to be anywhere else.

AFROZE: Oh.

AFROZE tries the hat on.

WHITNEY: Try the other one on?

AFROZE tries the other hat on.

Nope, see, I was right: the first one looks better. It brings out your eyes more.

AFROZE: Thanks! Does it make me look more like a guy?

WHITNEY: Kinda.

AFROZE: Cool. Hey, I never asked you. About where you'd wanna go if you could go anywhere else.

WHITNEY: It's okay, doesn't matter.

AFROZE: I'd like to know.

WHITNEY: Why?

AFROZE: Why not? I feel like I don't know that much about you.

WHITNEY: Oh, uh . . . I don't—really like talking about myself.

AFROZE: Is that why Noah always talks about himself?

WHITNEY: What?

AFROZE: I just kinda always hear him talking a lot.

WHITNEY: Well some people talk more than others. You don't talk a lot.

AFROZE: I do. When people talk to me.

Beat.

WHITNEY: You know, you can walk home with me and Noah if you want. You live really close to us.

AFROZE: Okay.

WHITNEY: Keep the hat. Don't tell anyone you got it from the lost and found. Isn't this Eli's lunch bag?

> *AFROZE shrugs their shoulders. WHITNEY takes the lunch bag and leaves. AFROZE ponders for a bit.*

AFROZE: *(to audience)* Lost and found . . . Hmm . . . Hey, can you give me my letter back? I gotta tell Shamsu about this!

WHITNEY: GO TO PAGE 109
AFROZE: GO TO PAGE 109

Wudu (Jihad)

JIHAD performs wudu quickly.

JIHAD: Okay, okay, I lied. You know I've never kissed anyone before, but I just wanted to sound like I knew what I was talking about a bit, you know? I wonder what it would feel like. I shouldn't lie, but it feels like everyone is lying. Like Eli is totally lying about what he sees when he closes his eyes. Should I try closing my eyes and see what happens?

JIHAD closes his eyes and thinks about someone but gets embarrassed.

Sorry, that's weird! The point is, just cuz he's lying doesn't mean I should lie. I should—well, there's a lot of things I should do, but I don't do them . . . like speaking Arabic. I should be able to, but I can't. I never learnt. My parents never taught me. You know what, I also shouldn't talk while I'm doing this. Oh, this is wudu. It's like a pre-prayer cleansing ritual. I gotta restart. Wanna join me?

GO TO PAGE 109

Speech Prep (Tara)

TARA organizes her bag quickly and writes in her journal, preparing for her student-rep speech. She takes a big swig of water before she begins writing. She makes some minor edits, then she asks the audience for advice.

TARA: Do you ever have those days or weeks or months, even, when nothing is going right? Ugh, you know what, I just need to refocus. I'm almost done my class-rep speech. I need to work on that.

As she takes out her speech, a card falls out.

Oh. That's . . . Okay, so, I'm writing this for Whitney. I mean it's pretty obvious her grandma being sick is making her really sad and even though she's always mean to me, I think a card like this will actually make her happier, because having your grandma sick can be really scary and I think that this will make Whitney feel like she's not alone cuz I'm basically gonna get the whole school to sign it.

And I think if she's happier around me, she'll be nicer. Sometimes, I know it's silly, but sometimes I think we could actually be really good friends. I've tried like . . . to show how nice I am, but nothing's really worked. I don't know.

Hey! Can you help me make the card?

Dear Whitney, I'm so sorry that your grandma is sick. I hope this card makes you feel better because all of us are thinking of you!

Love, Tara

GO TO PAGE 109

Punching a Wall (Eli)

> *ELI rages. It's violent and loud, but completely silent. He tenses his body as he screams silently at the wall, to himself, in his bag. It's wild and exaggerated but he takes care not to hurt or damage himself or anything around him. It's almost like he's thrashing around in a soundproof glass box. If he lets any of the sound out the bad feelings become real. He does everything he can to keep it inside. It goes on until he finds a place of stillness. Despite his best efforts, he starts to weep a little bit.*

ELI: *(whispering)* I just want my best friend back. Sorry. Can you guys . . . come with me to class?

Thanks.

GO TO PAGE 109

AAARHHHHH

Noah Needs to Talk (Noah)

NOAH: I can't do this anymore! This is exactly why I didn't want to go back to school! EveryTHING is different, everyONE is different, Eli is different. I knew talking to him again would change everything. He sat on my headphones, he kicked my neck, and he doesn't even care about me—all he wants to do is talk about Caleb and how great he is . . . or was, or about the night he died. But I don't want to think about that anymore. It's all I think about when I'm alone or at home—even when I try to force my brain to think anything else, the night Caleb died just keeps popping into my brain like a movie and there is no remote to press stop.

And why is Eli still trying to be my friend at school? Why now? He has his girlfriend Tara now so he shouldn't be trying to hang out with Whitney and me. He has his friends and I have mine. Nothing needs to change. I just want things to stay the way they were.

I'm going to tell you something . . . I used to think, before all of this happened, that I had a crush on Eli. He would make me laugh harder than anyone and he gives the best hugs. But that was at the beginning of the summer before all of this. Obviously he hypnotized me or something because there is no way I could crush on him . . . especially after seeing him lock lips with Tara and her mayo-breath mouth.

I just think I need my big brother. I need to talk to him. Sometimes I forget that he's not here and I'll run into his room to tell him something funny or go to yell his name and I catch myself before I get too far ahead of myself. It's like it's happening all over again and I remember I'm alone. I need to talk to him.

GO TO PAGE 109

14

Student-Rep Speech

The class files in with AFROZE *coming in last.*

Fantasy: AFROZE *walks in slow motion, like they're in a Bollywood rom-com college class and all the students turn to look. Everyone responds with dramatic noises such as "ooooo" or "wow."*

NOAH: Cool hat.

ELI: Afroze looks dope!

Everyone nods and agrees.

ALL: *(except* AFROZE*)* Mmmhhmm!

The fantasy ends.

They're each holding a recently marked math test. WHITNEY *and* TARA *did very well.* ELI *did not.*

WHITNEY: Hey, Noah, are you okay?

NOAH: Ya, I'm fine.

WHITNEY *knows that he's not, but she doesn't know what to say.*

TARA: Hey, Whitney, what did you get on your test?

WHITNEY: A. Why, what did you get?

TARA: Oh, um, an A-.

WHITNEY: What did you get, Eli?

ELI: Um . . . tests are stupid. It doesn't even matter.

WHITNEY: Okay . . .

TARA starts preparing for her presentation.

WHITNEY: *(to NOAH)* Oh, I forgot to tell you, Afroze is walking home with us.

NOAH: Ya, sure.

JIHAD: *(overhearing)* Wait, Afroze is walking home with you?

WHITNEY: Yeah, she lives right next to me.

JIHAD: How did you find that out?

WHITNEY: Duh, she just told me.

JIHAD: You don't speak Urdu?

WHITNEY: She's been able to speak English this whole time. Isn't that hilarious?

JIHAD looks at AFROZE and glares at them.

Ms. Hall approaches TARA's desk. TARA walks up to the front of the classroom.

Everyone listens (some more than others) while TARA *presents her student-rep speech.*

TARA: Good afternoon.

I'm talking to you today because I want to be your class representative. These are the reasons why:

I am a really good listener and I have heard all of your problems.

And I will start by speaking truthfully about what's possible and what's not possible to change at this school.

For example . . .

Fantasy: TARA *is standing at a podium. Everyone is listening attentively.*

If I become the next prime minister, I will make sure that Canada is a safe and welcoming place for all Canadians and newcomers. Canada is a multicultural nation, with many of us coming from many different places to share this one piece of land. I will work hard to make Canada a peaceful, kind, and loving place to live where all human rights are respected.

ALL: *(cheering)* Tara! Tara! Tara! Tara!

The fantasy ends.

TARA *has a coughing fit through the next part of her speech.*

These are just some of the many things I will do for our class and for the rest of the school should I be selected as class rep.

WHITNEY thinks TARA's failure is hilarious. To recognize this moment WHITNEY offers NOAH a handshake, which he rejects. He is looking at ELI.

WHITNEY: *(whispering)* Noah? Why are you staring at Eli?

ELI turns back and looks at NOAH.

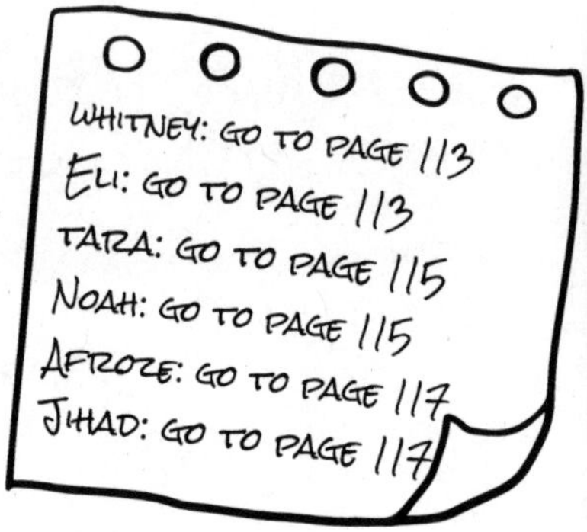

15A

Simultaneous Scenes

Checking In (Whitney and Eli)

ELI and WHITNEY bump into each other.

WHITNEY: Oh, hey, this is your lunch bag, right? I found it in the lost and found.

ELI: Oh, uh, thanks.

WHITNEY: Also, um, I want to talk to you.

ELI: About what?

WHITNEY: Well, I know you spent a lot of time with Noah over the summer and, like, I know I'm his best friend and everything, but we like literally haven't talked about what happened at all . . .

ELI: So?

WHITNEY: Is Noah okay?

ELI: What do you think?

WHITNEY: Ya, obviously he's not okay. I, um, I'm just wondering if I can help him now.

ELI: How would I know?

WHITNEY: You were there.

ELI: Ya, but he hasn't talked to me all year basically.

WHITNEY: Ya, I don't know what that's about.

ELI: I don't think he wants my help.

WHITNEY: He really cares about you.

ELI: He has a weird way of showing it.

WHITNEY: Sometimes I think you're the only person he really cares about.

Beat.

And I know he hasn't really been nice to you, but that's because he's really upset / and I'm just trying to—

ELI: I don't care.

WHITNEY: That's rude.

ELI: How? He's ignored me all year and you've been saying stuff about me and Tara, so why would I want to help either of you?

WHITNEY: He's really sad, Eli.

ELI: And I already said I don't care.

ELI: GO TO PAGE 120
WHITNEY: GO TO PAGE 121

I'm Really Sorry (Tara and Noah)

TARA and NOAH find themselves alone in the hallway. They have never been alone before. TARA musters up the courage to say what she wants to say.

TARA: Hey, Noah?

NOAH: Ya?

TARA: Will you sign this card for Whitney? It's because of her grandma.

NOAH: What about her grandma?

TARA: Well, you know how she's really sick.

NOAH: Oh, ya . . . that's really nice of you.

NOAH signs the card.

TARA: Also, I've been meaning to say this to you all year, but I'm really, really sorry about your brother.

NOAH: Okay . . .

TARA: I just mean, like, it's really shitty to have someone that you love die.

NOAH: Yup.

TARA: My vó died two years ago.

NOAH: Your who?

TARA: My vó. My grandma.

NOAH: Oh. Cool.

NOAH walks away.

TARA: Wait.

NOAH: What?

TARA: Did I do something wrong?

NOAH: No.

TARA: Okay. I just feel like you're mad at me.

NOAH: No, I just . . . I really didn't want to think about Caleb today.

TARA: I'm so sorry, Noah! I'm so sorry I brought him up.

NOAH: No. It's fine. It didn't work anyways.

TARA: What didn't work?

NOAH: Not thinking about him.

TARA: From what Eli tells me he was a really cool brother.

NOAH is unable to speak. He just nods and walks away. He needs a distraction. He needs to find WHITNEY.

TARA: GO TO PAGE 120
NOAH: GO TO PAGE 121

Muslim-Off (Afroze and Jihad)

In the prayer room. Silence.

Any time AFROZE *or* JIHAD *get angry in this scene, it is a quiet burning rage as they are also trying to be respectful of the room they are in.*

AFROZE: Hey. I'm really sorry.

JIHAD *doesn't respond.*

I'm sorry I didn't help out with the project. I can tell you about my family now if you–

JIHAD: I don't care.

AFROZE: Yeah you do. Otherwise you'd talk to me.

JIHAD: You can't just decide one day that you don't speak English and then decide the next that you do.

AFROZE: Ya, I know, but it's been really hard–

JIHAD: Plus Muslims don't lie, so how can you even say you're Muslim?

AFROZE: So you've never lied before?

JIHAD: You come to school with a scarf on your head and then you decide you want to wear that stupid hat! How Muslim is that?

Beat.

AFROZE: You know what, you don't even know anything about me.

JIHAD: I don't know anything about you because I didn't understand you.

AFROZE: You know, when I found out there was a prayer room in this school, I thought that was the one place I might actually feel welcome—where I could feel safe—because I am Muslim.

JIHAD: I don't think you belong here. Just go hang out with your new friend.

AFROZE: What new friend?

JIHAD: Whitney, obviously.

AFROZE: Why do you care if I'm friends with Whitney?

JIHAD: I don't, obviously

AFROZE: Yes you do. See, now you're lying.

JIHAD: I'm not lying!

They both stare each other down.

Fantasy: a Bollywood sound chimes, indicating a fight.

They fight. AFROZE *tries to use their dupatta as a weapon. There is a tug of war. There is pushing and pulling. They wind up grappling on the ground. They lie on the ground beside each other, exhausted.*

CONTINUE ON . . .

1 5 B

Pre Truth or Dare

JIHAD: How did you get Whitney to like you?

AFROZE: What?

JIHAD: It's just—you're so weird and Whitney's cool.

AFROZE: Thanks

JIHAD: Seriously. What did you do?

AFROZE: I didn't do anything.

JIHAD: But she thinks you're friends.

AFROZE: We are friends.

JIHAD: So I want to know how you did it!

AFROZE: Why do you care so much about what Whitney thinks? Maybe she just doesn't want to be your friend.

AFROZE walks away.

☆ ☆ ☆

AFROZE: GO TO PAGE 123
JIHAD: GO TO PAGE 123

TARA walks up to ELI. From the start they are awkward with each other.

TARA: Hey!

ELI: Hey.

TARA: Um . . .

ELI: Ya?

TARA: Can you sign this card for Whitney?

ELI: Why?

TARA: Her grandma's really sick right now and I thought it would be nice if we all signed a card for her.

ELI: Oh. Uh, I guess. But why do you have do it?

TARA: I don't know. I just wanted to be nice.

ELI: Okay . . .

He signs the card. There is awkward silence.

Soo . . . uh . . . Can we talk about . . . Wait, never mind.

TARA: What?

ELI: Oh, um . . . Did you really get an A on the algebra test?

TARA: Um, yeah.

ELI: Oh, what uhhh I don't know, I . . . I, I was just like wondering like how you studied for it cuz I, uh, well—oh I heard lots of people failed—I mean I didn't do so well but I didn't—okay, well actually—

TARA: Did you wanna come over this weekend and study for the next one? Nalisha's also coming.

ELI: Oh, no, I think I'll be okay.

TARA: Are you sure? My mom can make caldo verde again!

ELI: No, I'm good, thanks.

TARA: Are you sure?

ELI: Yeah, Tara, I'm fine, seriously. Just forget I said anything, okay?

TARA: Okay.

TARA: GO TO PAGE 123
ELI: GO TO PAGE 123

CONTINUE NOAH AND WHITNEY'S STORY HERE!

WHITNEY: Where were you?

NOAH: Oh, I was just talking to Tara.

WHITNEY: About what?

NOAH: Nothing really.

Pause.

Let's do something fun.

WHITNEY: Wanna play grounders?

NOAH: No, we did that yesterday.

WHITNEY: We can re-enact Tara's student-council speech.

NOAH: Um, no. Maybe later.

WHITNEY: Okay . . .

Beat.

They begin speaking simultaneously:

Um, we could just talk if you don't want to play anything?

NOAH: Oh, hey, um, I didn't know about your . . . Tara told me about your–

WHITNEY: What did she tell you?

NOAH: Oh, uh, nothing. I want to do something fun.

WHITNEY: Okay, ummm . . . We could play Truth or Dare.

NOAH: Yes! Who should we ask to play?

NOAH and WHITNEY look around.

CONTINUE ON . . .

1 6 A

Truth or Dare

WHITNEY: Jihad, Afroze, Truth or Dare.

JIHAD: Um, I don't really wanna play with–

NOAH: Jihad, shut up, come on.

AFROZE: What's Truth or Dare?

WHITNEY: It's really fun. You get to hear everyone's secrets and you have to do whatever someone tells you to do.

NOAH: So we have–

> *NOAH counts how many people are in the circle and then looks around.*

Hey, Tara, wanna play Truth or Dare?

TARA: Um, okay! Eli, do you wanna play?

ELI: Um . . . no, not / really . . .

TARA: Come on! You'll have fun!

NOAH: Okay, hurry up! Okay, hey, everyone, so we're playing Truth or Dare. I think Whitney should go first.

WHITNEY: Okay. Um . . . Tara, truth or dare?

TARA: Truth.

WHITNEY and NOAH whisper to each other, deciding what to ask TARA.

Hey, that's cheating!

WHITNEY: Not it's not. Is it true that you think you're going to lose to Alice Woo? And if so, how will your boyfriend Eli support you in the aftermath of the big loss?

The second question is not something NOAH and WHITNEY just discussed.

TARA: The results haven't come in yet. But Alice Woo is really cool, and she's got a great platform, but so do I. So I think it's a very tight race. And Eli is not my boyfriend.

Beat.

Whitney, truth or dare?

The way the scene continues depends on what the audience encourages each character to choose.

If WHITNEY is encouraged to choose "dare":

WHITNEY: Dare.

If WHITNEY is encouraged to choose "truth":

WHITNEY: Truth.

TARA: I dare you to take that mop and broom bend with your eyes closed while standing on one leg.

WHITNEY hesitates or struggles a bit at first, but then does it.

WHITNEY: And that's how you get on the soccer team.

TARA: Is it true Ms. Hall gave you five detentions last year?

WHITNEY: Ya, so?

The scene continues:

WHITNEY: Afroze, truth or dare?

If AFROZE is encouraged to choose "dare":

AFROZE: Dare.

WHITNEY: I dare you to swim around and make fish sounds.

AFROZE is embarrassed but enjoys themself.

If AFROZE is encouraged to choose "truth":

AFROZE: Truth.

WHITNEY: Who was your best friend in Pakistan?

AFROZE: Shamsu.

AFROZE: Tara, truth or dare?

TARA: Truth.

AFROZE: Ummm . . . What do you do after school?

TARA: Oh well most times I'll take the bus home and sometimes I'll get picked up and then I always make myself and my siblings an after-school snack and, um, when my parents get home they check to make sure I've done my homework and if I've gotten any / marks back–

WHITNEY yawns loudly.

Jihad, truth or dare?

If JIHAD is encouraged to choose "dare":

JIHAD: Dare.

TARA: I dare you to burp the alphabet.

If JIHAD is encouraged to choose "truth":

JIHAD: Truth.

TARA: Is it true you can burp the alphabet?

JIHAD: Yes.

The rest of the group screams, "Do it! Do it! Do it!"

JIHAD does. At first it's cool, then it gets uncomfortable. People are afraid he's going to vomit.

At this point TARA tries to get some audience members to sign WHITNEY's card. When speaking to the audience TARA says, "I know Whitney's been mean, but it's because her grandma's sick."

JIHAD: Noah. Truth or dare?

If NOAH is encouraged to choose "dare":

NOAH: Dare.

JIHAD: I dare you to do the splits

NOAH does the dare.

If NOAH is encouraged to choose "truth," JIHAD can ask one of two questions:

JIHAD: Is it true you used to do Irish dancing?

NOAH: No, my brother did.

JIHAD: Oh, I thought I saw a picture . . .

NOAH: That was my brother.

JIHAD: Is it true you like boys?

NOAH: Ya.

JIHAD: Oh, cool.

NOAH: Eli, truth or dare?

NOAH consults with WHITNEY.

If ELI is encouraged to choose "dare":

NOAH: I dare you to tell us what BEDMAS means.

ELI: *(with the help of his audience)* Brackets, exponents, division, multiplication, addition, and subtraction.

WHITNEY: If you know it so well why did you fail the math test?

If ELI is encouraged to choose "truth":

NOAH: Is it true you failed your math test?

ELI doesn't respond either way.

TARA: Hey, I think we should have an option to pass.

WHITNEY: Silence says all . . .

ELI: Whitney, truth or dare?

If WHITNEY *is encouraged to choose "dare":*

WHITNEY: Dare.

ELI: I dare you to go over to Noah's house since you've never been.

WHITNEY: That's stupid. I can't go over to his house right now.

ELI: Well how come you've never been over?

NOAH: My parents are weird–

If WHITNEY *is encouraged to choose "truth":*

WHITNEY: Truth.

ELI: How come you've never been over to Noah's house if you're his best friend?

WHITNEY: *(this takes a lot out of her)* He never asks me.

NOAH: That's because my parents are weird–

WHITNEY: Eli, truth or dare?

If ELI *is encouraged to choose "dare":*

ELI: Dare.

WHITNEY: I dare you to tell Noah what you said to me in the hall.

If ELI *is encouraged to choose "truth":*

ELI: Truth.

WHITNEY: What did you tell me about Noah in the hall?

ELI: Nothing.

NOAH: What did you say?

ELI: She asked about what happened in the summer.

It's very awkward. No one knows what to say. TARA *tries to save the day. She asks you:*

TARA: Hey, do you wanna play? What's your name?

YOU respond.

WHITNEY: No, it's Eli's turn.

ELI: Fine. ____________________, truth or dare.
(insert your name here)

If you choose "dare":

ELI: I dare you to shout that you love Ms. Hall.

If you choose "truth":

ELI: Is it true that you made out with a tree?

You do the dare or answer the truth, then continue the game.

YOU: *(prompted by NOAH)* Afroze, truth or dare?

If Afroze is encouraged to choose "dare":

AFROZE: Dare.

YOU: I dare you to show us your birth certificate.

AFROZE: Why?

NOAH: Because you're adopted!

AFROZE: No I'm not!

If Afroze is encouraged to choose "truth":

AFROZE: Truth.

YOU: Is it true that you're adopted?

AFROZE: No!

NOAH: Jihad, you were wrong.

WHITNEY: We knew it.

AFROZE: Jihad, truth or dare?

If JIHAD is encouraged to choose "dare":

JIHAD: Dare.

AFROZE: I dare you to tell me who put you in charge of the prayer room?

If JIHAD is encouraged to choose "truth":

JIHAD: Truth.

AFROZE: Who put you in charge of prayer room?

WHITNEY: Oh, Ms. Hall did.

There's general agreement among the classmates. JIHAD nods with them.

TARA: It was like two years ago. / You weren't here.

AFROZE: Isn't Islam supposed to be accepting?

JIHAD doesn't say anything. It is clear this question has affected him.

WHITNEY: Afroze, you can pick another person since Jihad isn't co-operating.

TARA: This isn't even how you play the game. The point is to get to know people.

WHITNEY: Tara, stop interrupting.

AFROZE: Okay, Noah, truth or dare?

NOAH: Truth.

AFROZE: Do you think your brother dying has made you feel more alive?

NOAH: I don't know.

Beat.

WHITNEY: I don't want to play anymore. It's almost time to get back to class anyways.

16B
Post Truth or Dare

The following scenes happen simultaneously as they travel to class.

Whitney and Noah

As everyone gets up, WHITNEY checks in with NOAH.

WHITNEY: Are you okay?

NOAH: Ya, I'm fine.

WHITNEY: I'll tell Afroze not to bring him up / again–

NOAH: No, don't! Just leave it alone.

WHITNEY: I know how upset it makes you–

NOAH: I don't want to talk about this anymore.

He pushes her away.

WHITNEY: GO TO PAGE 135
NOAH: GO TO PAGE 135

Tara and Afroze

TARA approaches AFROZE to sign WHITNEY's card.

TARA: Hey, Afroze? I made Whitney a card cuz her grandma's sick. I think she would really like it if you signed it.

AFROZE: Are you sure Whitney wants you to tell everybody about her grandma? She seems really private.

TARA: Well, it's tradition here to give someone a card when something sad, or good, happens.

AFROZE: *(hesitantly)* Okay.

AFROZE signs the card.

TARA: GO TO PAGE 135
AFROZE: GO TO PAGE 135

Jihad and Eli

JIHAD and ELI are the first ones in class.

An awkward silence.

JIHAD: I'm surprised Tara's not the first one here. Isn't student rep being announced now?

ELI: Why do you care?

JIHAD: I don't.

ELI: Okay . . . Don't make her feel bad if she loses.

JIHAD: Why do you care?

ELI: I don't.

JIHAD: Does this mean she really is your girlfriend?

ELI: Shut up.

Breaking news: Alice Woo is the new class rep!

You are the first to know. Do you want to tell ELI *or* JIHAD *first?*

CONTINUE ON . . .

17

Before School Presentations

JIHAD: Hey, everybody, guess what! Alice Woo is our new class rep! Woo!

NOAH: *(quietly to TARA)* Sorry.

TARA starts gathering her notes as a way to deal with losing.

TARA: Are you prepared for the presentation? Ms. Hall said we're going first.

WHITNEY: I know.

ELI: Hey, can we just go over some stuff so / I know we're on the same page about the presentation?

TARA: Sooo . . . Can I quiz you? I think it can help us both focus.

NOAH: What do you / wanna know?

WHITNEY: Okay, whatever.

TARA: What are my brother's names?

WHITNEY: Manuel, Matteo, Iago, and . . .

ELI: Uh, well, actually . . .

WHITNEY: Christopher.

NOAH: What??

TARA: Where did my parents immigrate from?

WHITNEY: Lisbon, Portugal. Specifically Belém.

TARA: Oh, great.

WHITNEY: Well this was useful.

ELI: I'm just not sure what to say about Caleb.

Beat.

JIHAD: What did you write about me?

AFROZE: Nothing.

JIHAD: What do you mean?

TARA: I'm not gonna talk about your grandma but I am gonna mention her. That's okay, right?

AFROZE: I didn't do it.

ELI: Hey, sorry I brought it up, / but I kinda need to know what I'm saying there otherwise . . .

WHITNEY: Yeah, it's fine.

JIHAD: Afroze, are you serious???

TARA: Okay, great. Um . . .

ELI: Noah?

JIHAD: That's really messed up cuz you understood everything I was saying when we were working together so why didn't you do it?

NOAH: I, I don't know what to say about Caleb either.

NOAH starts breathing heavily.

TARA: I wanted to give you this / because I think it'll make you feel better.

ELI: It's okay, it's okay, Noah . . .

JIHAD: You want me to fail?

ELI reaches for NOAH's hand. NOAH takes ELI's hand.

WHITNEY: What is that?

AFROZE: No, it's not that. It's not about you.

JIHAD: Yes it is! Why didn't you do your presentation???

ELI: We'll figure it out.

TARA: It's a card I made for your grandma. I got a lot of people / to sign it.

To my friend Whitney, I'm sorry you're going though such a rough time. I'll always be here for you. Love, Jihad

You're friends with Tara now? Okay . . . But also sorry to hear about your grandma.

Daphne

Sorry. —Eli

As your class president i will make sure you can have as many days off of school as you need to take care of your grandma.

Officially, Alice Woo, class president

Dear Whitney,

I am not sure this card will make you feel better, but it is nice to see that everyone has written in it. Change is hard.

Afroze

I heard your grandma is sick . . .
that's really sad —Nalisha

Nalisha and Daphne told me your grandma is sick and I just want to say I should have heard about it first. —Madeline

Dear Whitney, I'm so sorry that your grandma is sick. I hope this card makes you feel better because all of us are thinking about you!

Love, Tara

Tara made me sign this . . . but also it really sucks about your grandma.

Love, Noah

Hey Whitney, I'm really bummed that your grandma is dying. I always have an extra bag of Cheetos if you want to talk about it.

Marco

WHITNEY: You told other people about my grandma???

TARA: Oh . . . I thought–

AFROZE: I don't care about school, / especially not here.

WHITNEY: No, I don't want that. I don't want people to know about my stuff!

WHITNEY takes the card and crumples it. Ms. Hall approaches.

She, she wrote a card and I didn't– No, I'm not being dramatic, I– But . . .

Swimming Sequence

The students try to run out of the ocean but they keep getting knocked over by waves.

18

Simultaneous Scenes

Outside Bathrooms (Eli and Afroze)

ELI comes out of the boys' bathroom and nearly knocks into AFROZE, who looks as if they are about to go in.

ELI: Whoa. Hey.

AFROZE: Oh. Hi. Um. I was just . . . Looking at the door.

ELI: Oh. Awesome.

AFROZE: What's it like in there?

ELI: It's just . . . normal. I hear there's a couch in there. *(points to girls' washroom)*

AFROZE: Oh . . . no.

ELI: Okay, I gotta go.

ELI starts to leave.

AFROZE: Hey. Um . . . You won't tell anyone about me looking at the door, right?

ELI: Nope. It's cool. I look at doors all the time.

AFROZE laughs. This makes ELI laugh too.

Hey, I like the new hat. It's dope.

AFROZE: Thanks. It's, uh, from the lost and found.

ELI: No way! Sucks for the kid who lost it.

AFROZE: Ya, Whitney found it for me. When she found your lunch bag.

ELI: Oh, right.

AFROZE: Um, so, was the question I asked Noah in Truth or Dare okay?

ELI: I dunno.

AFROZE: He seemed to be having a hard time in class just now.

ELI: Why does everyone always ask me about Noah?

AFROZE: Well, because, you know, you're . . .

ELI: What?

AFROZE: You guys are . . . don't you like him?

ELI: Oh, um . . .

ELI walks away.

AFROZE: GO TO PAGE 150
ELI: GO TO PAGE 150

Heartbeat (Noah)

NOAH is feeling his heartbeat, trying to calm it down.

He does that until his heart rate slows.

He is trying to remember a different heartbeat.

He taps it out on his leg.

NOAH: Have you ever put your head on someone's chest and heard their heartbeat? Or have you ever felt how when you are excited, or nervous, or scared your heartbeat changes and you can feel the rhythm and the pattern change? Or put your fingers on your wrist and felt a pulse? Are you ever scared that you won't remember the sound of someone's heartbeat?

I think I've started to forget what Caleb's sounds like. The other night I was thinking about how Caleb and I used to run as fast as we could in the backyard and then we would see whose heart was beating faster and his would always beat the same beat. But I couldn't remember the beat. I tried everything, tapping out the sound, saying the sound–thump-thump, thump-thump . . . no that's not it. Thump-thump-thump, thump-thump-thump . . . no, that's not it either! I even tried listening to the clock tick but it wasn't the same pattern.

I got so frustrated and scared that I started to panic in my room. Because I'm already forgetting things. What if I don't remember? What if I forget how he sounds, or how he smells, what his voice sounds like, or what if I forget his laugh? His laugh is my favourite sound. I'm so scared he's going to vanish from the videos in my head and that I won't remember.

How do you make sure you don't forget? What do you do?

Do you have someone important in your life that you think about all the time? Can you tell me a story about them?

WRITE ABOUT SOMEONE THAT IS IMPORTANT TO YOU

LUDE A
WING/
HOTO

GO TO PAGE 150

Panic Attack (Tara)

Tara: What's happening? Nothing is going like I thought it would. No, I can't focus on this right now!

Ahh! I thought I was doing the right thing. People seem to like it when other people care about a sad thing in their life. When my vó died two years ago I was really sad for like a month and nobody knew why.

And then she just started saying all the facts about my family—and she knew everything—and I knew that my presentation wasn't as good and that I was going to fail. I can't fail, I can't fail.

I can't fail. I can't fail. How did Alice Woo win student rep?! She failed a grade! She literally failed! And all she did was promise more pizza lunch, which is so stupid. I actually had a platform. I actually cared. I care so much!

I care about soccer but I can't even make the team. How did that happen? All my brothers made the team so easily. They think I'm so stupid and pathetic I can't even make elementary school soccer team. And now I have to tell them I'm not class rep and I'm failing history. I mean, not yet, but after walking out on the presentation there's no way I'm gonna not fail history. Why can't I do anything? What's wrong with me! Okay, focus . . .

I can't go home now. My parents will be so mad. They think I'm going to be prime minister one day, but you can't be prime minister if you fail. You can't be anything if you fail . . . How did Alice Woo win!?

TARA crumbles into a small ball and breathes, thinks, trying to calm down. She drinks some water. TARA tries her best to pull herself together.

Whatever. It can't get worse from here. Focus.

TARA hears the school bell.

Oh no . . . It's time for the school dance. Can you come with me?

GO TO PAGE 150

Jihad Pleads His Case (Jihad and Whitney)

JIHAD stops WHITNEY in the hallway.

JIHAD: Hey, Whitney!

WHITNEY: Hey.

JIHAD: That was a really weird class, eh?

WHITNEY: Ya.

JIHAD: Um . . . So . . . Hey, um, I was wondering if I could talk to you. I mean, umm, ask you a question really quickly . . .

WHITNEY: What's up?

JIHAD: I heard that you gave that hat to Afroze.

WHITNEY: Well I found it more than gave it to her . . .

JIHAD: Cool, cool. Um, well you and I have been talking more this year—I mean we always talked, but, ya, anyways— I mean . . . so maybe you want to hang out sometime? You can come over—my dad makes really great pizza when people come over. We have this really cool wood-burning oven and . . .

Fantasy:

WHITNEY: JIHAD!!!

JIHAD: WHITN-AY!!!

JIHAD and WHITNEY perform the ultimate handshake of JIHAD's dreams.

The fantasy ends.

Pause.

WHITNEY: Oh, um, ya. We can hang out sometime.

JIHAD: Awesome, so . . .

WHITNEY: Ya, well, I gotta go. See you at the dance.

JIHAD: Ya.

WHITNEY walks away.

Oh, uh, Whitney?

WHITNEY: Ya?

JIHAD: That was really uncool what Tara did. Getting everyone to sign the card for your grandma behind your back.

WHITNEY: Ya, thanks.

JIHAD: But also it sucks that your grandma's sick.

WHITNEY: Ya.

WHITNEY walks away.

CONTINUE ON . . .

19

School Dance/Dance Battle

All of the students enter the school dance. NOAH, WHITNEY, *and* AFROZE *group together.* JIHAD, TARA, *and* ELI *are standing alone. They all stick close to the wall.* NOAH *and* ELI *look at each other, clearly affected by what just happened leading up the to the school presentations.*

Fantasy: JIHAD *is the centre of attention and he is* AMAZING. *Everyone cheers him on. When he does a certain move everyone yells, "*HOT DOG!*"*

The fantasy ends.

WHITNEY *schemes with* NOAH, JIHAD, *and* AFROZE *(who isn't into it) to push* ELI *and* TARA *together.* TARA *and* ELI *both drag their heels, resisting the push. Just as they are about to meet . . .*

Fantasy: NOAH *and* ELI *shyly ask each other to dance and they hold each other, both awkward and happy. The other students sway around them.*

The fantasy ends.

ELI *and* TARA *are slow-dancing and it is very awkward. They can't make eye contact. Everyone else is standing around gossiping*

and looking on, feeling awkward themselves. NOAH *is particularly uncomfortable.* ELI *and* TARA *make eye contact and . . .*

Fantasy: Everyone dances like no one is watching. They are carefree. They are wild, they scream, grunt, roar. A wave crashes over them and . . .

The fantasy ends.

TARA *and* ELI *continue dancing awkwardly.* NOAH *approaches* WHITNEY.

NOAH: I don't think we should have pushed them together. They're clearly really uncomfortable.

WHITNEY: Ya. But they're dating, so it doesn't matter.

NOAH: No they're not! Tara kissed him, but I don't think Eli liked it.

WHITNEY: How do you know? You're not even friends with him.

NOAH: I just know.

WHITNEY: How?

NOAH: It doesn't matter.

WHITNEY: Okay, so can you stop freaking out now? This is funny.

NOAH: No it's not. You're a bully.

WHITNEY: Excuse me?

NOAH: You heard me.

NOAH walks away from WHITNEY.

WHITNEY: Say it again.

NOAH whips around and . . . IT'S ON! It's time to dance battle. WHITNEY and NOAH challenge each other, each trying to one up each other with their dance moves.

It's not enough. They each need a team. WHITNEY recruits JIHAD and AFROZE and NOAH recruits ELI and TARA. The teams of three battle, going back and forth, the dance moves getting better and better.

It's still not enough. They need you.

Whose team are you on? What dance moves would you use for the battle?

Everyone joins in and it's chaos. It's the best dancing this school has ever seen.

AFROZE is pushed forward to initiate a dance move. They stand there awkwardly, unsure what to do.

Fantasy: AFROZE breaks into a fully choreographed Bollywood dance. The rest of the students join in as their backup dancers, executing Bollywood dance moves and exuding the corresponding facial expressions. They lift AFROZE up in a glorious movie moment.

The fantasy ends.

AFROZE is still frozen with everyone looking at them, expecting them to offer a dance move. WHITNEY saves the moment by landing in the splits, which no one else can do. She has won.

20

Note Passing

All of the students are paying attention to the lesson Ms. Hall is teaching. They care to varying degrees (some take notes, some try not to fall asleep, etc.). NOAH, *meanwhile, is writing a note.*

The note says:

WHITNEY HAS SAID THIS ABOUT YOU:

Eli: Your moms are embarrassed because your grades are so low.

Tara: The world would be a better place if you weren't born.

Jihad: You will never be cool. You're a permanent loser.

Afroze: You're an evil ghost who curses people because you're really sad.

I KNOW IT SUCKS TO READ THIS, BUT IT'S BETTER THAT YOU KNOW THE TRUTH. SORRY.

He passes the note to ELI. *Once he does this the whole class takes notice. When* ELI *is done reading the note he looks at* WHITNEY *and then* NOAH *indicates to pass it to* TARA. TARA *is conflicted between listening to the teacher and reading the note. Finally her intrigue is too much and she takes the note from* ELI. *As she's reading the note she glances at* WHITNEY. *Now it is* VERY *obvious that the note is about* WHITNEY. WHITNEY *indicates to* JIHAD *that he should get the note from* TARA *to pass to her.* JIHAD *indicates to* TARA *that she should pass him the note and she does because she thinks he needs to read the note.* JIHAD *opens the note to read it before he gives it to* WHITNEY. *He chooses not to believe what the note says, but as he's passing it* WHITNEY, NOAH *and* ELI *lunge and* NOAH *gets the note. Ms. Hall turns at the noise and they all have to cover up what just happened.* NOAH *passes it to* ELI, *who passes it to* AFROZE. AFROZE *doesn't care about the note, so they don't pass it to anybody. The entire class lunges for the note and there is a battle.* AFROZE *gets shoved to the floor and they all end up in awkward positions.* WHITNEY *gets the note. They all turn sharply to Ms. Hall, who has finally noticed what is going on. Ms. Hall walks over to* WHITNEY*'s desk and* WHITNEY *quickly eats the note.*

WHITNEY: What are you talking about, Ms.? There isn't anything going on . . . But, Ms., I can't miss any more soccer practice . . . Everyone else was involved too . . .

Fantasy:

WHAT? What did I do this time? No, seriously, tell me. There was a note being passed around by the ENTIRE class—about me—and somehow I'm gonna get in trouble for it? Why? Why me? Why always me? Do you hate me? I just want you to leave me alone. I'm tired. Why always me? Just say it. Just say it. Just say it.

Silence.

The fantasy ends.

Okay, fine. I'll see you after school.

21

Cafeteria

NOAH, ELI, and TARA sit together. JIHAD and WHITNEY sit together. AFROZE sits alone. Nobody is talking. It is really awkward and tense.

TARA: Why are you staring at me?

WHITNEY: I'm not staring at you. I'm staring past you.

NOAH: I'm surprised you're even hungry.

WHITNEY: Why?

NOAH: I thought you'd be full after all that paper you just ate.

WHITNEY: *(to TARA)* Why aren't you sitting with your boyfriend?

TARA: He's not / my boyfriend.

ELI: I'm not her boyfriend.

NOAH: Whitney, can you drop this?

WHITNEY: Why, are you jealous?

NOAH: No.

TARA: He's not my boyfriend. Why does everyone keep bringing this up?

JIHAD: Because you kissed him.

TARA: So, it didn't mean anything.

ELI: Then why did you kiss me?

TARA: I don't know. I didn't think it would be a big deal.

ELI: Clearly it was a big deal. Look at what happened at the dance.

NOAH: *(to WHITNEY)* Ya, you shouldn't have / pushed them together.

TARA: Eli, you know that wasn't my fault.

WHITNEY: *(to NOAH)* You were there too.

AFROZE: We all were.

ELI: We've never even talked about it.

NOAH: Yes, / but only one of us said what was written in that note.

TARA: Can we talk now?

JIHAD: You exaggerated. Whitney's not actually that mean.

NOAH: / Wanna bet?

TARA: Yes she is!

AFROZE: But you guys don't even actually know her.

TARA: / Yes we do, Afroze.

NOAH: Trust me, I know / alllll about her.

WHITNEY: No you don't. You don't know / what I'm going through.

TARA: *(to AFROZE)* It's okay, / you don't understand.

ELI: All right, great, so I guess we're just never / gonna talk about why you kissed me.

NOAH: *(to WHITNEY)* What is that supposed to mean?

WHITNEY: You haven't asked about my grandma once this year. You haven't been there for Eli / either, so you're mean.

AFROZE: *(to TARA)* Stop talking to me like I don't know anything.

NOAH: Whatever. Eli and I are friends now.

JIHAD: Well, Afroze, you gotta admit it's a little hard keeping up with / what you know and don't know.

WHITNEY: Oh don't worry, Afroze, / when Tara talks like that, it just means she's trying to control everything.

ELI: Wait. No we're not.

TARA: No I'm not.

AFROZE: *(to JIHAD)* You would know things about me if you took the time to listen.

JIHAD: You don't even know yourself!

WHITNEY: *(to TARA)* That's all you ever do.

ELI: You ignored me all year.

WHITNEY: You try to control situations that are way out of your control / to get people to like you.

JIHAD: You're wearing a scarf on your head one day and then wearing a guy's hat the next.

AFROZE: So what?

TARA: Whitney, you do realize you have the most control in the school, right? Everyone wants / to be your friend.

NOAH: Well–I was dealing with stuff.

JIHAD: So, so, sometimes–

ELI: You still are. You're still wearing Caleb's jersey.

TARA: But you don't open up to anyone. You're just mean all the time. Why would you act like that, especially when . . .

WHITNEY: What???

ELI: And it's okay. You're allowed to feel–

NOAH: I DON'T WANNA FEEL SAD ANYMORE!

Magic: the students scream all their rage out. Back to reality.

JIHAD: Sometimes my sister feels scared when she's wearing the hijab outside and she can't just take it off. And I wore a thawb to school last year and NO ONE thought it was cool.

TARA: I see how Ms. Hall treats you.

NOAH: You can't even deal with all your feelings, so I don't need advice from you.

AFROZE: It's hard for me here too.

TARA: I think it's unfair.

JIHAD: Yeah, well, at least people notice you. You should care about that instead of pretending like nothing matters here.

ELI: Friends don't treat each other like this.

AFROZE: I notice you. I noticed you changing yourself to try to be cool.

ELI: Why did you stop talking to me?

TARA: I've always wanted to say something but–

WHITNEY: You're too busy following all the rules and trying to be perfect.

AFROZE: And even then, this whole year I wanted to be your friend.

WHITNEY: Just let go!

ELI: Why did you stop talking to me?

NOAH: Because, Eli, even though you were with me all summer, you have no idea what I've been through. What if I lose you too?

Swimming Sequence

The water crashes over the students like a waterfall. They stand there, letting the water wash over them, giving them strength.

NOAH: GO TO PAGE 163
JIHAD: GO TO PAGE 164
TARA: GO TO PAGE 165
ELI: GO TO PAGE 166
WHITNEY: GO TO PAGE 167
AFROZE: GO TO PAGE 168

22
The Reclamation

Removing the Shirt (Noah)

NOAH: I just wanted everything to be the same as it was. But everything has changed. It's like I think I'm happy for a split second and then something reminds me and the happiness is just gone. I don't know how else to react, so I just get sassy, because it's funny and it makes Whitney laugh and I stop feeling sad for a little while.

But it makes other people sad . . . It makes Eli sad. I am hurting my best friend's feelings because I don't want to feel anything.

I thought wearing Caleb's jersey to school would make me feel better. Kind of like armour. Like maybe if I wore it they would know not to bring him up. But it was worse when nobody talked about it.

I think I should take it off now.

> *NOAH takes off the jersey, folds it, and puts it back in the box of Caleb's things.*

I have to find Eli and apologize to him. I hope he forgives me . . . I don't want to lose him too. Have you ever had to apologize to someone? Can you tell me about it?

WRITE ABOUT A TIME YOU HAD TO APOLOGIZE TO SOMEONE

GO TO PAGE 17

Wudu Realization (Jihad)

JIHAD begins wudu in the same way he did before, but this time he is deeply impacted by what AFROZE said. It is slower, more reflective. He has a memory:

JIHAD: My favourite day of the week is Friday because that's when we go to our mosque. You know, I kinda recently realized that it's not the praying that gets me really excited, but it's the moment when we go in and the room is full of other Muslims from our neighbourhood. A lot of them are Lebanese, but there are so many other languages too. My dad says it's mostly Farsi and Urdu. There are people from all over the world, like Iran and Pakistan, and we're all there to pray. Because I've never been to Lebanon, sometimes when I picture what home looks like I picture all those people in the mosque. I also get to wear my thawb there, which I love, and it's not weird because everyone's wearing one or something like it.

I really miss the summer when I got to go every day. I guess I have the prayer room here, but it's not the same. My mom told our teacher we had to pray in an empty classroom and that's how the prayer room started. First my sister Jahida was in charge, but when she graduated I got the responsibility. I stopped wearing my thawb though. Everyone here thought it was weird.

As JIHAD pours water over his head he begins to free himself from the pressure of trying to fit in. When he's done he puts on his thawb and grabs his old one for AFROZE.

GO TO PAGE 171

Unpacking (Tara)

TARA comes home and flings her stuff down. Her movement alternates between throwing stuff into her bag and unpacking her bag, repacking her bag, stuffing her things into the bag, pulling it all out to reorganize, and then eventually flinging her stuff everywhere and letting go of all the tension. She lies on the ground, surrounded by the mess of her things.

She is wrestling with the anxiety inside of her. Should she go back to the way she was before, or should she embrace the changing person she is becoming? These are the questions she is wrestling with in this movement sequence. In the end she decides to embrace the person she is becoming.

Tara: When I was first learning how to play soccer, my brothers said I had to be the water girl and just watch for a few games. I was really serious about being the water girl, because it was intense and important. But I also really wanted to play. Then during one game it started to rain and I ran into the middle of the field and just threw myself into the game. I don't even know what I was thinking. I just wanted to have fun. My vó always used to say rain makes everything grow, not just plants and flowers but like people too. The last time we gardened together, it was raining so much, but we didn't stop. We stayed in the rain and got soaked. We couldn't stop laughing.

Pause.

I don't really think I've had fun since I started taking things so seriously?

GO TO PAGE 169

Discovery (Eli)

ELI can't contain it any longer. He has the same quiet explosion as before, but the feelings are twisting and knotting him up like he's possessed by a ghost or an alien. And it's winning. He writhes without a sound until everything comes up like word vomit.

ELI: Oh god, I like him. I really, really like him. Afroze was right. I like Noah. He's rude and mean and cute and sweet and a big jerk and its weird being around him because my chest feels empty and heavy at the same time. I hate how much I like him! WHY GOD. WHY HAVE YOU DONE THIS TO ME. Do you ever just want to hold hands with someone and not say anything. Just like be there?

He imagines it and gets goosebumps.

Whewf! Awwww, man. And then there's the whole Tara thing?! Like, what even was that?! I mean, I still like her, but I don't like her like her like I like Noah. And I wish I could've talked to Noah about this but nooooooo(ah), he had to be a little drama queen and—no. You know what? I'm gonna go talk to him. I'm gonna. Go. Talk to him. Yeah? Yeah! No, I'm not— YES. NO. YES. YES. OKAY, ALL RIGHT. Forget it, let's just go while I gots the guts. Let's go. Come on. Hype me up. LET'S GO. Before I bail.

GO TO PAGE 169

Whales (Whitney)

WHITNEY: Did I ever tell you what my favourite whale is? Well I think it's the orca—you know, the killer whale—but lately I've been researching the baleen whale. They are one of the largest known animals to have ever existed, which means they're pretty powerful. They can swim really fast—with the fastest able to travel at thirty-seven kilometres per hour. Baleen whales have rarely been kept in captivity because their large size makes them difficult creatures to trap.

You know what I've been dreaming about recently? I keep having the same dream over and over. In my dream I'm a baleen whale and I've made my rare trip up to the surface. I can't turn my head because whales have infused neck vertebrae, making it hard to see what's around them, but I know that my grandma is above me, high in the sky, maybe in a hot air balloon, watching the magnificent morning light glitter on my skin. She feels far away, but also close. I spray water out of my spout and somehow it reaches her all the way in the clouds. It's my way of letting her know I'll be okay. I always wake up feeling both really happy and really sad.

I haven't told anyone about this dream even though I'm having it every night and I think about it all the time. I feel like I want to, but I also feel like once I talk about it it'll be like an oil spill in the ocean—impossible to contain.

Maybe that's why Noah and I haven't been able to talk about the hard things all year. Because once we start maybe we could never stop and we won't be the same. Okay, I can't stay here forever.

WHITNEY goes.

GO TO PAGE 170

Dear Shamsu (Afroze)

Dear Shamsu, aap kaisi hain?

I have so much to tell you!

Meh har din aapko yaad karti hoon likhen phir bhi, I'm sorry I took so long to write to you!

Every day I hope you don't forget about me, or hate me.

I'm wearing this cool hat right now that Whitney—she's this girl in my class—she helped me pick it out from this special place called the Lost and Found. It's a boy's hat. And Eli—he's a boy in my class—he might give me a tour of the boys' bathroom next week. Aap yeh sab believe kar sakti hain?? You were the first person I ever told about how confused I felt. But now I feel like I found people here who I can also tell about those things.

Yahan pey, it hasn't all been great. I've made some mistakes too. Like not writing to you sooner.

Likhen mujhe patha hai ke hum milenge phir se, Chenab River ke paas, and we'll see whose toes will get prunier in the water!

Meh Allah se mangti hoon the best best best always for you.

I feel so different now but hamesha hamesha yours, Afroze.

GO TO PAGE 171

2 3
After Reclamation

These scenes happen simultaneously. JIHAD *and* AFROZE'S *scene plays out until the next scene.* ELI, TARA, WHITNEY, *and* NOAH'S *scenes switch halfway through.*

Eli and Tara

ELI: Tara!

TARA: Hey, Eli.

ELI: I gotta tell you something. I . . . felt really confused after you kissed me. I wasn't sure if we had to start dating or something after or if it meant nothing, or if we were still gonna be friends after or not . . . So all of that was really confusing and it sucked that we didn't really get to talk about it and it sucked that you seemed okay with that . . . Sorry if this is a lot. I just want you to know how I feel. Felt. Feel.

TARA: Thanks for telling me, Eli. I didn't know. Well I knew something was wrong . . . I'm sorry.

ELI: It's okay.

TARA: And just so you know, I don't have a crush on you. And if you ever wanna talk or you need anything, can you just let me know? I'm trying to do this thing where I don't tell people what they need to do all the time. Okay?

ELI: Okay.

Beat.

I need math help.

TARA: Okay.

ELI: Thanks, Taradactyl!

TARA: Rawr!

TARA: GO TO PAGE 174
ELI: GO TO PAGE 173

Whitney and Noah

NOAH: I know you're mad at me.

WHITNEY: I'm not mad at you. Well, I'm not anymore. I just . . . I was so worried about asking you about your brother that I was afraid to tell you how I feel about my grandma being sick.

NOAH: It's my fault for never asking you. Can I ask you now?

WHITNEY: Okay.

NOAH: How do you feel about your grandma being sick?

WHITNEY: I don't know. It feels like I feel everything.

NOAH: I know. I've been so angry. And sad. And mean. It sucks.

WHITNEY: How do you deal with it?

NOAH: I'm not doing a really good job.

WHITNEY: I don't think I'm gonna do a good job either.

NOAH: Maybe next year we'll be different.

WHITNEY: Unless we both fail and gotta re-Woo everything.

They both laugh, kinda awkwardly.

NOAH: Okay, um, I have to go.

WHITNEY: Okay. See you around.

NOAH: GO TO PAGE 173
WHITNEY: GO TO PAGE 174

Jihad and Afroze

AFROZE is folding up their letter and putting it in an envelope when JIHAD interrupts them.

JIHAD: Can I ask you something?

AFROZE: Umm . . .

JIHAD: Why do you like to be alone all the time? Just a question.

AFROZE: Sometimes I do. And sometimes when it looks like I'm alone, it doesn't feel like I am.

JIHAD: Oh. Like, because you're with ghosts or . . . ?

AFROZE: No. Um, it's kind of like my friend Shamsu is always with me. Because I'm always thinking of her.

JIHAD: Cool. Um. You know, a lot of people don't know this about me, but I think a lot about cooking and how I'm gonna try cooking more next year, like my dad, like that's something I'd like to do, especially specifically deep-dish pizza.

AFROZE: Yeah. I've noticed you eat a lot of pizza.

JIHAD nods.

JIHAD: Um, you know, a lot of people also don't know this, but I think I'm gonna ask my sister to teach me Arabic. I don't know why I didn't think of that before.

AFROZE: Well, it takes time to know things.

JIHAD: Right. Um. I'd like to try your food again, if you ever had extra. I'd obviously trade you. We could sign a trade agreement, kinda like the one Lebanon and Pakistan have with each other.

AFROZE: Oh . . . But I'm from Europe.

JIHAD: What??

AFROZE shakes their head then laughs. JIHAD laughs too.

AFROZE: Hey, I never asked. How mad were your parents when they had to sign on your presentation mark?

JIHAD: They were fine.

AFROZE: Really?

JIHAD: Yeah . . . My sister signed on their behalf. They were . . . too busy.

AFROZE: Wow, your sister seems . . . dope.

JIHAD: Yeah . . . She's the best. She can pretty much teach you how to play every video game that's ever existed basically, if you're interested. She plays games made for girls and for boys and games for like everyone, so you could choose . . .

AFROZE: Thanks . . .

JIHAD: Actually, you know, there's this corner in the prayer room that's kinda tucked away right by the tiny window and it's really good for reading, or writing letters. Or you could do whatever . . . In the prayer room.

AFROZE: Oh. Thanks.

JIHAD: Also, if you still want to keep coming, you could wear this.

AFROZE looks at JIHAD, who smiles. AFROZE curses JIHAD. They both laugh.

AFROZE: GO TO PAGE 176
JIHAD: GO TO PAGE 176

Noah and Eli

NOAH is sitting in a hallway corner. ELI joins him.

NOAH: Are we talking now?

ELI nods.

Okay. Um. You don't have to forgive me right now, but I hope one day you will, but I just want to say I am really sorry. I know that I hurt you, and I hurt Whitney too, and I'm not really sure why . . .

Pause.

ELI: Well I kicked you in the neck.

They both laugh. Then, another moment of silence.

I wanna say how I feel. I'm sad when we don't talk. And I think it'd be really awesome if we could be friends like how we were before the school year started.

NOAH: Okay. Yes. I think so too. Okay. Yes.

ELI: I don't want to feel alone anymore.

NOAH: I'm here.

NOAH and ELI nervously explore holding each other's hands. They finally touch and they find comfort in that. They make each other laugh because they are nervous. Tentatively, they kiss.

ELI: GO TO PAGE 176
NOAH: GO TO PAGE 176

Tara and Whitney

Outside the change rooms.

TARA: Ugh, it feels like we've been swimming so much this year.

WHITNEY: Yeah, maybe they're trying to prepare us for when the whole world turns into an ocean.

TARA: That's a scary thought.

WHITNEY: Or maybe it'd be cool. I love being underwater, but I hate swimming lessons.

TARA: Wow, seriously? You're the best swimmer in the class. I really hope we don't have to do laps today. All I want to do is just splash around.

WHITNEY: No excessive splashing, remember.

TARA: I can't focus on that rule right now. I just want to be free.

Beat.

WHITNEY: Hey, uh . . . next time Ms. Hall says something to me, I'm going to say something back. I don't know what yet. Will you back me up?

TARA: Ya.

CONTINUE ON . . .

24

Swimming

All of the students stand around the edge of the pool in their bathing suits. They are still awkward and self-conscious in their swimwear, especially with the people they just made new connections with. They have been through a lot together. Everything is changing.

Fantasy: the students see the wave approaching, and this time they run right into it.

Acknowledgements

The *Eraser* team would like to thank the following people and organizations without whom the project would not have become what it is today:

Lynda Hill, for seeing *Eraser*'s potential.

Tom Arthur Davis and Why Not Theatre's RISER Project for giving us our first opportunity.

Lisa Marie DiLiberto and Theatre Direct for believing in the project and supporting us in achieving our vision.

Our student audiences for being in the story with us and making the world of the play come to life with such energy and effortlessness.

Nightwood Theatre and Roseneath Theatre for supporting us with space and their personal time. Thank you to Andrew Lamb for crying every time he saw the show!

Why Not Theatre and Roseneath Theatre for giving us the resources to make our work on the published script possible.

Playwrights Canada Press for helping us honour the choose-your-own-adventure style of the piece and letting us have so much fun with this publication.

The Toronto Arts Council, the Ontario Arts Council, and the Canada Council for the Arts for funding the development stages and production run.

Lo Fine, for being our magical personal transportation service.

Marina Gomes would like to thank:

Tony and Sharon Gomes for valuing the importance of storytelling and never letting me feel like I was alone growing up.

Ariana, Amelia, and Ethan Gomes, it is an honour to be a part of the core four. Your motivation and love inspire me every day. Tara would have been lucky to have grown up with you.

David Hudyma for being in my corner and pushing me to find the joy in everything while never losing sight of what's important.

The *Eraser* Team for bringing me in and for striving to make people feel seen through our art. With you the world becomes a better place.

Nathan Redburn would like to thank:

John and Cindy, my parents, for your unwavering support and love. To my co-creators, family, and friends, thank you for your encouragement and inspiration—each of you has played a vital role in this journey.

About the Authors

Bilal Baig (she/they) is a writer, actor, and producer for stage and screen, as well as a workshop developer and facilitator for art-focused non-profits. Baig's published works include their first play, *Acha Bacha* (2020, nominated for the Dayne Ogilvie Prize from the Writer's Trust of Canada), and an anthology of monologues they co-edited for queer/trans artists titled *This Is Beyond* (2023). Baig was a co-creator, executive producer, and lead actor in their Peabody Award–winning series *Sort Of* (2021–2023), for which Baig received the Canadian Screen Award for comedy writing and performance, as well as a Gotham Award nomination for performance in a new series. Baig has facilitated creative writing and playwriting programs for trans artists, BIPOC artists, and trans youth, including Trans Gemmes (2019–2020), Paprika Festival's Playwrights Unit (2019–2023), Being Me (2023–), and Dialogue Dolls (2023–).

Sadie Epstein-Fine (they/them) is multi- and interdisciplinary creator based in Tkaronto (Toronto). Sadie has trained in dance, devised theatre, classical theatre direction, musical theatre creation, and playwriting and their work is a fusion of that training. They are also a future dreamer, creating the world they want to live in through their artistic practice. Sadie's work has amplified queer, trans, and queerspawn voices, including the anthology *Spawning Generations: Rants and Reflections on Growing Up with LGBTQ+ Parents* (Demeter Press, Nominated for Lambda Literary and Forward Indies Awards, named a top 10 book of 2018 in *NOW*

Magazine), which they co-edited, and the Queerspawn Digital Storytelling Project in partnership with the ArQuives. Directing and choreography credits include *The Sound of Music* (Nightwood Theatre), *The Dybbuk* (Toronto Metropolitan University), *Eraser* (The Riser Project/Why Not Theatre, nominated for five Dora Mavor Moore Awards, including Outstanding Direction and New Play), *Eraser: A New Normal* (Theatre Direct), and *Mamma Mia!* (Nightwood Theatre).

Christol Bryan is a first-generation Canadian artist of Afro-Caribbean descent. Her work uses the experiences of her life and family to tell meaningful stories that resonate in a continued effort to bring people from all walks of life closer to a common understanding. Christol is a performer who has training in clown, contemporary vocal, and physical theatre techniques.

Born in Toronto, Marina Gomes is a graduate of the University of Windsor B.F.A. acting program. As an actor/creator, Marina has trained with members of the SITI Company, Festival Players Academy, and was a Young Innovator at Nightwood Theatre. Marina shares her passion for theatre and learning as an artist educator with various companies throughout the GTA. Selected acting credits include Lexi in *Lexi and the Flying B's* (Toronto Fringe), Tara in *Eraser* (Eraser Theatre), and Tara in *Eraser: A New Normal* (Theatre Direct).

Yousef Kadoura was born in the midwestern United States and raised in Ottawa, Ontario. He is a Lebanese Canadian actor, writer, and producer, as well as a right leg below knee amputee. Yousef is a graduate of the 2017 acting program at the National Theatre School of Canada. Yousef is also a founding company member of Other HeArts, a new performance collective. As an artist Yousef seeks to draw from a plurality of experiences and disciplines to expand the boundaries of performance in pursuit of accessibility, presence, and shared experience.

Tijiki Morris was raised in Pakistan and came to Canada at eighteen. They co-created and led the puppetry collective Artichoke Heart, where they directed and devised pieces including *We Walk Among You* and *Cirqular* (Les Trois Jours de Casteliers, Montreal Fringe, Best of Fringe Toronto and Beyond the Mountain). Their play *Rootless* was presented at the SummerWorks Performance Festival and Theatre Passe Muraille's Buzz Series. They were a selected artist for the inaugural Loughborough Lake Writer's Retreat with Crow's Theatre and Mongrel Media. Tijiki has been an artist-in-residence at Theatre Passe Muraille, Mermaid Theatre, Cahoots Theatre's Hot House Lift Off Playwrights' Unit, and was named as one of "30 Cahoots theatre makers who will shape the next 30 years of Canadian Theatre."

Anthony Perpuse mostly goes by Tony and uses he/him pronouns. He is a Toronto-based Filipino Canadian actor who received his B.F.A. in Performance Acting from the (then called) Ryerson Theatre School in 2016 and was awarded the Perry Schneiderman Comedy Award. Some of his theatre credits include *Theory* (Tarragon Theatre), *Eraser* (Eraser Theatre), *Through the Bamboo* (Uwi Collective), and *Orestes* (Tarragon Theatre), while film credits include *Workin' Moms, Save Me, The 5th Estate,* and *Run the Burbs* (CBC); *VHS '94* (Hangar 18); and *The Handmaid's Tale* (HBO). He received a Dora Mavor Moore Award nomination in 2019 in the Theatre for Young Audiences Division for Outstanding Production, Outstanding New Play, and Outstanding Ensemble with Eraser Theatre (for this play!).

Nathan Redburn is a multidisciplinary actor and creator from the small farm town of Arthur, Ontario, with an affinity for devised theatre, performance creation, improv, sketch comedy, and writing. Nathan takes inspiration for characters he creates and in his writing from his hometown and his own lived experiences. Nathan left Arthur in 2012 to pursue acting at York University, where he received his B.F.A. from York's Acting Conservatory. Since graduating in 2017 he has gone on to perform in shows across Toronto, which have garnered him several Dora Mavor Moore Award nominations. Nathan has also found his stride in writing, acting for film and television, and further creating in the realm of performance art.